DOPOSTORIA

Christoph Keller

BOM
DIA
BOA
TARDE
BOA
NOITE

PREFACE

Seen from the perspective of an archive, all memory is the memory of something deceased, and all culture builds on memory of the past. Thus in exploring archives, we are worshipping death and inhabiting a cemetery that is the history of culture. Is there no way out? Archaeology raises questions about memory and its activation. In which ways do we refer to art history as a cultural legacy of the past? Are Western museum archives and their re-collections of cultural heritage a cult of the dead—and if so, are we inhabiting a necropolis? What options do we have to navigate within them or out of them? How can archives, together with other ways of storing and retrieving knowledge, be adapted to our present needs?

This book evolved from a research project posing these questions, which I was invited to pursue as an artist fellow at the Bibliotheca Hertziana, the Max Planck Institute for Art History in Rome. What most attracted my interest at the institution was the Fototeca, the immense Photographic Collection from the history of art and architecture, which has been an important element in the development of this renowned research center. The points of departure for my research were the subject areas of *Roma / Antichità* and *Roma / Urbanistica* within the digitized part of the archive's photographic holdings, which are subdivided both geographically and thematically.

The idea of "history" is messianic, since it has a defined beginning, a starting point—which may be set, for instance, in antiquity or at the beginning of linear writing—and its drive is to move onward toward an abstract future, which is located beyond the stratigraphy of this history. Photography is a history-producing machine.

Every photograph makes a mark in the historical timeline at the moment it is taken, which from then on disappears continuously and relentlessly into the drain of pastness. What comes thereafter would be post-history: *dopostoria*.

Dopostoria is a notion for what comes after history, meaning after a linear historiography. It is a paradoxical concept insofar as it refers back to history itself. When Pier Paolo Pasolini introduces this term in his poem "Io sono una forza del Passato," he does so from the viewpoint of an artist of language, who senses the confinements of this history, or more precisely, of a present that has carried the burden of this past since antiquity. As an artist, he self-consciously stumbles through the ruins of this past, surmising the advent of a time when these words will have lost their meaning.

The threefold result of my endeavors as a researching artist, if one ventures to speak of "research results" in the field of art at all, is documented in this book. It presents, as the first outcome of the research project, a description of an as-yet-unpublished and somehow unfinished film in five acts—a cinematic fragment, so to speak. This fragment is largely composed of visual material taken from the research subject, the photographic archive of the Bibliotheca Hertziana. As a filmic collage, it relies on moments of silence, snippets of voices, and rough transitions, as well as on rhythms and superimpositions, whereby only some sequences are accompanied by excerpts of music.

The second outcome comprises a series of twenty-six collages, or superimpositions, each based on photographic material from the collection. As a series of images, they can form a spatial installation invoking the vast and abstract photo archive, with its hundreds of thousands of images, thereby rendering it palpable. The superimpositions are inverted in color, partly solarized, and visually processed, thereby detaching themselves from their previous archival photographic sources—that is, from the mimetic aspects of their photographic existence—and thus allowing them to resonate as a series (see the plates at the end of this book). On a semantic level, these images refer to the meta-archive of the original negatives: the last physical witnesses of the moments and situations depicted in the respective photographs. The collages are relatively small in size, therefore enabling intimate contemplation. They constitute showcases of a phantasmagorical Rome and simultaneously pictorial windows into their archive of origin.

The third outcome of the research is this small book itself—not only as a repository of textual and visual information but also as an object that conceives and contains its own book form; as an object with its possibilities, to pass from one hand to another, to be flipped through, to be read only partially or as a whole, to travel, or to just sit and wait.

PREFAZIONE

Vista dalla prospettiva di un archivio, tutta la memoria è la memoria di qualcosa defunto e tutta la cultura si costruisce sulla memoria del passato. Così veneriamo la morte e viviamo in un cimitero che è la storia della cultura. E non c'è una via d'uscita? L'archeologia solleva domande sulla memoria e la sua attivazione: in che modo ci relazioniamo alla storia dell'arte come retaggio culturale del passato? Gli archivi dei musei occidentali e le loro raccolte sono forse un culto dei morti? E se così fosse, viviamo quindi in una necropoli? Quali opzioni abbiamo per navigare al suo interno, o per uscirne? Come possono quegli archivi, nei modi di immagazzinare e recuperare la conoscenza, essere adattati ai nostri bisogni attuali?

È a partire da queste domande che nasce questo libro, sviluppato grazie ad un percorso di ricerca che ho svolto in qualità di artista ricercatore presso la Bibliotheca Hertziana – Istituto Max Planck per la storia dell'arte, a Roma. Ad attirare la mia attenzione verso questa istituzione fu in particolare la Fototeca: l'immensa collezione fotografica di storia dell'arte e dell'architettura che rappresentò un elemento chiave nello sviluppo del rinomato centro di ricerca. Il punto di partenza del mio studio sono state le aree tematiche "Roma/Antichità" e "Roma/Urbanistica", e la parte digitalizzata del patrimonio fotografico dell'archivio, suddiviso sia per area geografica che per tema.

La nozione di Storia è messianica poiché ha un inizio definito da un punto di partenza – fissato, ad esempio, all'inizio della scrittura lineare – e la sua spinta è quella di andare sempre avanti, verso un futuro astratto che si trova oltre la stratigrafia di questa storia. La fotografia è una macchina sfornastoria. Ogni fotografia lascia una traccia sulla linea del tempo nel momento in cui viene scattata. Da quel momento in poi essa scompare continuamente e inesorabilmente giù per lo scarico del passato. Quel che avviene dopo sarebbe la post-storia, ovvero la "dopostoria".

La dopostoria è una nozione che riguarda ciò che viene dopo la storia, ossia dopo una storiografia lineare. È un concetto paradossale nella misura in cui si riferisce alla storia stessa. Quando Pier Paolo Pasolini introduce questo termine nella sua poesia *Io sono una forza del Passato*, lo fa dal punto di vista di un artista del linguaggio, che avverte i confini di questa storia, o più precisamente, di un presente che porta il peso di un passato fin dall'antichità. Come artista, Pasolini inciampa consapevolmente tra le rovine di questo passato, ipotizzando l'avvento di un tempo in cui queste parole avranno perso ogni significato.

Il triplice risultato dei miei sforzi come artista-ricercatore è documentato in questo libro, sempre che sia lecito azzardare la definizione "risultati di ricerca" nel campo dell'arte. Il libro presenta, come primo risultato, la descrizione di un film in cinque atti ancora inedito e in qualche modo incompiuto – un frammento cinematografico, per così dire. Questo frammento è in gran parte composto da materiale visivo tratto dall'oggetto stesso della ricerca: l'archivio fotografico della Bibliotheca Hertziana. Come un collage, il film si basa su momenti di silenzio, frammenti di voci, transizioni brusche, ritmi e sovrapposizioni, così come su di alcune sequenze accompagnate da brani musicali.

Il secondo risultato comprende una serie di ventisei collage, o sovrapposizioni, ognuno basato su materiale fotografico della Fototeca. Alla stregua di una galleria di immagini, essi vanno a comporre un'installazione che invoca il vasto e astratto archivio fotografico, con le sue diverse centinaia di migliaia di immagini, rendendolo così tangibile. Le sovrapposizioni sono a colori invertiti, editate, ed in parte solarizzate, così da prendere le distanze dalle loro precedenti fonti fotografiche d'archivio – e dunque dagli aspetti mimetici della loro esistenza fotografica – permettendo loro di risuonare come serie (vedi le tavole alla fine di questo libro). A livello semantico, le immagini fanno riferimento al meta-archivio dei negativi originali: gli ultimi testimoni fisici dei momenti e delle situazioni raffigurati nelle rispettive fotografie. Di dimensioni relativamente ridotte che ne permettono una contemplazione intima, i collage costituiscono piccole finestre su una Roma fantasmagorica, offrendo sguardi pittorici sul loro archivio d'origine.

Il terzo risultato della ricerca è questo stesso piccolo libro – non solo come deposito di informazioni testuali e visive ma anche come oggetto concepito e contenuto nella propria forma di libro – un oggetto pieno di possibilità, che può essere passato di mano in mano, sfogliato, letto parzialmente o per intero, che può viaggiare, ma anche rimanere fermo in attesa.

DOPOSTORIA – A CINEMATIC FRAGMENT IN FIVE ACTS

The film consists of five chapters or acts, each announced by intertitles with the numbers 1 to 5. It begins with the title of the film—DOPOSTORIA—in white letters on a black background, without translation. Three languages are used: Italian, German, and English. The film's title is part of the work and illuminates it. *Dopostoria* is a film about history in the double sense of the Italian word *storia*, which can signify a *history* as well as a *story*. It is a work about photography, or more precisely, about the life arrested in it, which confronts the idea of history. Pier Paolo Pasolini's poem "Io sono una forza del Passato" served as an inspiration.[1]

Dopostoria was conceived as a film about history, based on the holdings of the photo archive of Bibliotheca Hertziana, the Max Planck Institute for Art History in Rome. The intertwining of different languages and national histories

1. In Pier Paolo Pasolini's poem "Io sono una forza del Passato" (I am a force of the Past), from 1962, the word *dopostoria* appears to describe the premonition of a transition about to take place. Here is an excerpt:

> Giro per la Tuscolana come un pazzo,
> per l'Appia come un cane senza padrone.
> O guardo i crepuscoli, le mattine
> su Roma, sulla Ciociaria, sul mondo,
> come i primi atti della **Dopostoria**,
> cui io assisto, per privilegio d'anagrafe,
> dall'orlo estremo di qualche età sepolta.

(I walk around on the Tuscolana like a madman / along the Via Appia like a stray dog / Or I contemplate the twilight of the morning hours / over Rome, over the Ciociaria, over the world / like the first acts of **post-history** / which I witness through the privilege of the moment of my birth / from the very edge of a buried age).

suited this purpose, not just as a case study, but because history cannot be grasped as a whole; rather, it is found in relationalities and the overlapping of interpretations. Accordingly, there is a dilemma inherent in art history, since it belongs neither entirely to the field of art nor entirely to that of history and must therefore constantly reassure itself of both domains.

The Italian compound word *dopostoria*[2] echoes the concept of "post-history" as used by the media philosopher Vilém Flusser: not as an age after history that will dawn one day but as a description of the present, the now.[3] In this light, the references to Walter Benjamin's *Theses on the Philosophy of History* become recognizable.[4] Preparing myself for the topic, I read works such as *Infanzia e Storia* and *Creazione e Anarchia* by Giorgio Agamben, which address the role that art plays in actualizing the past,[5] and *Sputiamo su Hegel*

2. Composed of *dopo* (after) and *storia* (history, story).

3. "The invention of photography is just as decisive an historical turning point as was the invention of writing. With writing, history as such begins as the struggle against idolatry. With photography, 'post-history' begins as a struggle against textolatry." Vilém Flusser, *Towards a Philosophy of Photography* (Göttingen: European Photography, 1984), 12.

4. "The here-and-now, which as a model of messianic time summarizes the entire history of humanity into a monstrous abbreviation, coincides to a hair with the figure, which the history of humanity makes in the universe." Walter Benjamin, *Theses on the Philosophy of History* (1940), trans. Dennis Redmond (2005), https://www.marxists.org/reference/archive/benjamin/1940/history.htm.

5. "Since obviously the only place where the past can live is the present, if the present is no longer aware of its past as living, then universities and museums become problematic places. And if art has today become for us an eminent figure—perhaps the eminent figure—of this past, then the question that we must never stop posing is: what is the place of art in the present?" Giorgio Agamben, *Creation and Anarchy*, trans. Adam Kotsko (Stanford, CA: Stanford University Press, 2019), 7.

by Carla Lonzi,[6] which attacks the Marxist concept of history, from a feminist perspective, via its grounding in Hegelian dialectics.[7]

I

The film *Dopostoria* begins with a color photograph as an opening image—the only picture in the work that I took myself. It shows the view from the cemetery on the Aeolian island of Lipari across to the Rocca Rossa, a red rock formation by the sea with ancient fortifications and an archaeological museum.[8] The photo does not remain unchanged, however, but slowly transforms, as if in the developer bath of an analog photo lab: first into its own reversal color negative and then further, until it appears as a black-and-white negative image.

The double gesture of returning to its own negative alludes to the analog photographic process in which the original negative bears testimony to the initial photographic act.[9]

6. "Let us consider the man–woman relationship in Hegel, the philosopher who saw the slave as the driving moment of history. He rationalized patriarchal control most subtly of all within the dialectics of a divine feminine principle and a human masculine principle. The former presided in the family, the latter in the community." Carla Lonzi: *Let's Spit on Hegel*, trans. Veronica Newman (Milan: Scritti di Rivolta Femminile, 1977).

7. "In all these respects art, considered in its highest vocation, is and remains for us a thing of the past." G. W. F. Hegel, *Hegel's Aesthetics: Lectures on Fine Art*, vol. 1, trans. T. M. Knox (Oxford: Clarendon Press, 1975), 11.

8. See image on cover.

9. "The only 'objective' truth that photographs offer is the assertion that somebody or something [. . .] was somewhere and took a picture." Allan Sekula, *Photography Against the Grain* (Halifax: Press of Nova Scotia College of Art and Design, 1984), 57.

In other words, it alludes to the moment when the photographic image was "cut out" of a historical situation in order to "capture" it and make it retrievable and available again.[10] The digital transformation of the picture into its own reversal image, taking place before our eyes, signals that the analog photographic original no longer exists, and that the mythical act of photographic image creation has disappeared—into the image processing programs, perhaps, but above all into the distribution of images through social and digital media platforms.[11]

In the first chapter of the film, Maria Clara Martinelli, an archaeologist at the museum in Lipari, talks about sepulchral cultures dating back to prehistoric times. She explains how the deceased then were either cremated or buried. In early clay grave vessels, the dead were often placed in a kneeling position. The vessels' bulging shapes, she says, recall a mother's belly and thus the connection between death and birth.[12] The film's images remain black here; only the voice of the archaeologist appears. It is the sound of the voice more than anything else that defines an individual: the fragile expression of being alive that already

10. "[. . .] one can't possess the present but one can possess the past." Susan Sontag, *On Photography* (New York: Rosetta Books, 1977), 128.

11. "The ancient magic is prehistoric, it is older than historical consciousness; the new magic is 'post-historic,' it follows on after historical consciousness. The new enchantment is not designed to alter the world out there but our concepts in relation to the world. It is magic of the second order: conjuring tricks with abstractions." Vilém Flusser, *Towards a Philosophy of Photography*, trans. Anthony Mathews (London: Reaktion Books, 2000), 17.

12. See Maria Clara Martinelli's contribution to this book, p. 63.

anticipates its later silencing. Toward the end of the film sequence, the archaeologist suddenly speaks about her own mortality.[13]

The non-image emphasizes the physicality of her voice. The subject here is something that lies beyond the image, beyond any imagination: death. First, it is about the deaths of others, as represented in funeral rites and mortuary rituals, which belong to the most ancient forms of human culture. Funerary culture, in this sense, refers to keeping the life and deeds of a late member of a community in remembrance so they can be used further. The connection between death and birth can be understood in this way: something is passed on. This is implied in the form of the grave vessels in which the dead are preserved in fetal positions: the deceased are ready for rebirth. Death itself, though, remains obscure. It is the other, unreachable shore. There is no image for it. Death is tied to the community; without any means for one's own life to transcend in some way to the next generations, there is no afterlife and thus no hope.[14]

13. "What can be said is bound to a superordinate instance—the voice—as an articulated pronouncement, *phone semantike*. But the voice is simultaneously inscribed with an irreducible negativity: that of the death of the speaker and the absence of who is invoked in language." Julian Nida-Rümelin and Elif Özmen, *Philosophie der Gegenwart in Einzeldarstellungen* (Stuttgart: Kröner, 2nd edition, 1999), 11.

14. "Death hides no secret. It opens no door. It is the end of a person. What survives is what he or she has given to other people, what stays in their memory." Norbert Elias, *The Loneliness of The Dying*, trans. Edmund Jephcott (New York: Continuum, 1985), 67.

II

The sequence of images in the second chapter begins with the pilgrimage church San Lorenzo fuori le mura and moves on from there to the adjoining municipal cemetery of Rome, the Campo Verano, a veritable necropolis with magnificent avenues and quarters for the dead of different social and political classes, and architectural preferences, mirroring the living city of Rome. Here, in the spirit of the Roman Baroque, the focus is on the facade, the exterior —only this time transposed to the time of the Italian nation-state—and less on the tombs' intimate contents.

The vocal score by Carlo Gesualdo da Venosa accompanying the images of the modern Roman cemetery sets a mood from an era that preceded its founding and lends the tomb photographs a meaning that lies beyond what appears in the images. Gesualdo's madrigal compositions are steeped in guilt and pain. They leave behind the harmony of early Renaissance music and herald the advent of the Baroque.

As the photo sequence continues, suggesting a walk through a deserted cemetery, it becomes increasingly apparent that it is composed of archival material. Each image bears the same stamp in the lower right-hand corner. Sometimes the labeled cardboard on which the photos are mounted can be seen. This introduces yet another context, one that no longer refers solely to the visible content of the images but also to their archiving.[15]

15. "The capacity for accurate description, the ability to establish distinct relations of time and event, image and statement, have come to define the terms of archival production proper to the language of those mechanical mediums, each of which give new phenomenological account of the world as image." Okwui Enwezor, *Archive Fever: Photography between History and the Monument* (New York: Steidl, 2007), 11–12.

Photo archives and the medium of analogue photography are closely related. Painting is collected, whereas photography is archived, at least initially. Photographs are powerful witnesses to a vanished past.[16] The film thus suggests a twofold connection: between the cemetery and the archive on the one hand, and between photography and death on the other; the cemetery as both a reflection and a silent antithesis of the city of Rome. The photographs are also mute—the depicted scenes have been deprived of their soundca silencing that is reiterated again and again, each time they are viewed.

Then another monochrome black screen appears, and a voice starts speaking in German. It belongs to the historian Carolin Kosuch, who talks about sepulchral cultures in the modern period and compares the gradual decay of the buried body with the "phasing out" conveyed by the Jewish mourning rite, both of which are parallel processes toward an increasing immateriality of death.[17]

III

The third and middle chapter is the core of the film, and was also its point of departure: the question of whether an immense cultural entity like the Photographic Collection of the Bibliotheca Hertziana in Rome can be depicted in its entirety in a film.

A photo archive is an abyss—or more precisely, a gigantic labyrinth—which cannot be easily surveyed and grasped

16. "Having a photograph of Shakespeare would be like having a nail from the True Cross." Susan Sontag, *On Photography*, 1977, 120.

17. See Carolin Kosuch's contribution to this book, p. 41.

as a whole. If a hypothetical film were to show every image of the collection for only one second each, it would have to run continuously for some ten days and nights before all of its archival images appeared. Although the number of images would soon exceed the viewers' capacity to remember them, visual analogies in the rhythmic stream of the photographic images would remain subliminally recognizable.

With this in mind, I first made a selection of images from the photo archive of the Hertziana, applying neither an objective method nor the principle of chance, but rather my own personal preferences and interests. Keyword searches for architectural monuments in Rome, such as "obelisco," "mausoleo," and also, for example, Mussolini's "Foro Italico," resulted in an initial batch of photographs in thematic groups with visual and contextual ties.

Then I assembled the images into film sequences, so that each photograph is superimposed first with the preceding one and then with the following one, that is, AB, BC, CD, DE, EF, etc. The rapid succession of images in thematic groups thus creates a kind of imprint of the archive, which benefits from the audience's ability to quickly apprehend image sequences as synoptic ensembles of different image typologies. It is a fast-paced, phantasmagorical journey of approximately seven minutes through Rome, and simultaneously through various sub-areas—"provinces"—of the collection.

THE OTHER OF THE ARCHIVE

The same holds true for an archive as for photography: they are both mute. But how can an archive be given a voice or a sound? First of all, this requires an audience, a counterpart. Ultimately, this question concerns the bodies associated with the archive and the body of the archive itself.

I wanted to overcome the torpor of the photo library's history, to set it in motion, to rhythmize it. This meant turning the archive, in which certain views on history are inscribed, into an object, into artistic material, thereby transforming it.[18] This transformation process, though, required neither admitting the continuity of the old in the new, nor adopting a categorical opposition to the existing, which would also consolidate the old. Instead, like a ghost, the absent Other of the archive should be allowed to appear.[19] Its contrasting apparition only has to be perceptible for brief moments in order to expose the archive for what it really is: an efficacious interplay of images and power relationships.

That the archive itself remains abstract means that it still has not attained a body of its own.[20] However, the project was not intended as a survey of a concrete series of images,

18. "… these petrified relations must be forced to dance by singing their own tune to them!" Karl Marx, *Critique of Hegel's Philosophy of Right* (1844), in *Marx and Engels Collected Works*, vol. 3 (London: Lawrence & Wishart, 1975), 178.

19. "Might there not be a *time for phantoms*, a return of the images, a "survival" (*Nachleben*) that is not subject to the model of transmission presupposed by the "imitation" (*Nachahmung*) of ancient works by more recent works? Might there not be a *time for the memory* of images—an obscure game of the repressed and its eternal return—that is not the one proposed by this history of art, by this narrative?" Georges Didi-Huberman, *The Surviving Image: Phantoms of Time and Time of Phantoms: Aby Warburg's History of Art* (2002), trans. Harvey Mendelsohn (University Park: Penn State University Press, 2016), 11.

20. "In structural terms, the archive is both an abstract paradigmatic entity and a concrete institution. In both senses, the archive is a vast substitution set, providing for a relation of general equivalence between images." Allan Sekula, "The Body and the Archive," in *October* 39 (Winter 1986), 17.

or of an individual archive, but rather of a system, of which the archive is but a symptom.

Concepts of history cannot be transformed from within, but must be presented in a radically different way.[21] Archives are never neutral but strive to preserve themselves. This poses a challenge for their artistic treatment. Whoever accepts the rules of an archive has already lost, or rather, can no longer evade its presuppositions. This is the logic of the archive.

Strictly speaking, the photo library of the Bibliotheca Hertziana—one of the world's leading art-historical photo archives, with a stock of more than 870,000 photographs, primarily of Italian art and architecture from late antiquity to the present—is not an archive but a *museum collection*, since the institution elevates the artworks depicted in the respective photographs as significant to art history through their inclusion in the collection. Conversely, this means that everything else that was also relevant for a particular movement or era, this Other, finds itself outside the collection and thus excluded from an art-historical canon that the institution establishes.[22]

Therefore, the only option was to break with the archive's prescribed rules of usage in order to adopt an artistic per-

21. Audre Lorde: "The Master's Tools Will Never Dismantle the Master's House," in *Sister Outsider* (Berkeley: Crossing Press, 1984), 110–113.

22. "The West would therefore remain unable [. . .] to conceive of an Other to what it calls human—an Other, therefore, to its correlated postulates of power, truth, freedom. All other modes of being human would instead have to be seen not as the alternative modes of being human that they are 'out there,' but adaptively, as the lack of the West's ontologically absolute self-description." Sylvia Wynter, "Unsettling the Coloniality of Being/Power/Truth/Freedom Towards the Human, After Man, Its Overrepresentation—An Argument," *CR: The New Centennial Review* 3, no. 3 (2003), 257–337, here p. 282.

spective on the histories it presents, to evoke that absent Other from within the archive—and at the same time, to provide access to the archive as a whole by transposing it in a quasi-ceremonial gesture from the present into the past tense—and to release it, altered in this way, back into the world: Dopostoria.

The image sequence of the third chapter is accompanied by an excerpt from a composition for several pianos by Julius Eastman.[23] Juxtaposing Eastman's music with canonical images of European art history sets a significant counterpoint to the legacy of the renowned institute for the study of Italian art in Rome. The archive has historically been limited to a mostly white, exclusively European perspective on art history, which long ignored that the conditions of what it excludes—such as exclusion, exploitation, slavery, and colonialism—are actually constitutive of it. Eastman's music is introduced here to contrast with the archive as its concrete Other, without expanding on its own legacy.[24]

23. See also the audiovisual composition *The Third Part of the Third Measure* (2017) by the artist collective The Otolith Group (Anjalika Sagar and Kodwo Eshun), which celebrates Julius Eastman's political and compositional work. http://otolithgroup.org.

24. "There is need to read Eastman's work not only within its musical sensitivity, structure or texture–(ar)rhythmic, (dis)harmony, phonic–but also consider Eastman as a political being who saw his work as a medium to deliberate on the sociopolitical, economy, religion, as well as issues of gender, race and sexuality. While race and sexuality were very important and played a primal role in Eastman's compositions, they were not the only topics Eastman dealt with, which is the impression one gets when one peruses articles and narrations about Eastman today. Especially with the rhetoric of the 'rediscovery' of Eastman within the music and visual art fields, which in itself sounds like giving light to darkness, Eastman is particularly portrayed–if not reduced–to his blackness and his gayness." Bonaventure Soh Bejeng Ndikung, "I Love to Love, Oh Pleasant Love. The Marvel of Julius Eastman," 2021. https://www.arsenal-berlin.de/en/berlinale-forum/archive/program-archive/2018/magazine/articles/the-marvel-of-julius-eastman/.

At the same time, this incongruity evokes some of what has been repressed throughout this art history, or rather its absence, which has now become apparent.[25]

Just as the film's photographic sequences are temporal expressions of a visual language—revealing rhythms, pauses, and moments of resistance—the musical excerpts work both with and against the logic of the archive, distancing and connecting elements simultaneously.

IV

The fourth chapter relates a story in short intertitles against a black background. Again, a voice (or rather its absence and reappearance) is placed at the center, as a silent "inner voice" that reads the flow of intertitles aloud. Formally, the fourth chapter draws on my earlier film *Anarcheology*, to which *Dopostoria* has ties. The personal story is about the fragility of life and begins with a dream.

25. "If we want to leave behind the representations and the unthought-of things resulting from this past [the colonial period], we need to work on the history and the imaginary of a relationship that itself still awaits decolonization." Felwine Sarr and Benedicte Savoy: *Zurückgeben. Über die Restitution afrikanischer Kulturgüter* (Berlin: Matthes & Seitz, 2019), 76–77.

DOPOSTORIA –
EIN FILMFRAGMENT
IN FÜNF AKTEN

Der Film besteht aus fünf Kapiteln oder Akten, die jeweils durch Zwischentitel mit den Zahlen von eins bis fünf angekündigt werden. Er beginnt mit dem Titel des Films „DOPOSTORIA“ in weißen Lettern auf schwarzem Grund, ohne Übersetzung. Es werden drei Sprachen verwendet: Italienisch, Deutsch und Englisch. Der Filmtitel ist bereits Teil der Arbeit und strahlt auf sie aus. *Dopostoria* ist ein Film über Geschichte im doppelten Wortsinn. Er handelt von Fotografie, oder genauer von dem in ihr eingefrorenen Leben, welches der Idee von Geschichte gegenübersteht. Pier Paolo Pasolinis Gedicht *Io sono una forza del Passato* stand am Anfang.[1]

Es sollte also ein Film über Geschichte werden, ausgehend von den Beständen des Fotoarchivs der Bibliotheca Hertziana, dem Max-Planck-Institut für Kunstgeschichte

1. In Pier Paolo Pasolinis Gedicht „Io sono una forza del Passato“ (Ich bin eine Macht aus der Vergangenheit) von 1962 beschreibt das Wort „Dopostoria“ die Vorahnung eines sich gerade vollziehenden Zeitenübergangs. Hier ein Ausschnitt:

> “Giro per la Tuscolana come un pazzo,
> per l'Appia come un cane senza padrone.
> O guardo i crepuscoli, le mattine
> su Roma, sulla Ciociaria, sul mondo,
> come i primi atti della **Dopostoria**,
> cui io assisto, per privilegio d'anagrafe,
> dall'orlo estremo di qualche età sepolta.”

(Ich laufe auf der Tuscolana herum wie ein Verrückter / entlang der Via Appia wie ein streunender Hund / Oder ich betrachte das Zwielicht der Morgenstunden / über Rom, über der Ciociaria, über der Welt / wie die ersten Akte der **Nachgeschichte** / denen ich durch das Privileg des Zeitpunkts meiner Geburt / vom äußersten Rand eines verschütteten Zeitalters aus beiwohne. Übers. d. Verf.)

in Rom. Die Verquickung verschiedener Sprachen und Nationalgeschichten kam mir dabei zupass, nicht so sehr als Fallstudie, sondern auch, weil sich nicht über „die Geschichte" im Allgemeinen sprechen lässt und sie sich vielmehr in Relationen sowie in der Überlagerung verschiedener Interpretationen wiederfindet. Dementsprechend wohnt auch der Kunstgeschichte ein Dilemma inne, da sie weder ganz der Kunst zugehört noch ganz der Geschichte und sie sich beider Felder stets aufs Neue vergewissern muss.

Das italienische Wort *dopostoria*, zusammengesetzt aus *dopo*=danach und *storia*=Geschichte, lässt den Begriff der *Nachgeschichte* anklingen, wie ihn der Medienphilosoph Vilém Flusser verwendet hat[2]: nicht als ein Zeitalter nach der Geschichte, das einst kommen wird, sondern als Beschreibung der Gegenwart, des Jetzt. Vor diesem Hintergrund werden auch die Bezüge zu Walter Benjamins Geschichtsfragment erkennbar.[3] In Vorbereitung auf das Thema habe ich mich durch einige Werke gelesen, wie zum Beispiel *Infanzia e Storia* oder *Creazione e Anarchia*[4] von Giorgio Agamben, in welchem die Rolle der Kunst für die

2. „Die Erfindung der Fotografie ist ein ebenso entscheidendes historisches Ereignis, wie es die Erfindung der Schrift war. Mit der Schrift beginnt die Geschichte im engeren Sinn, und zwar als Kampf gegen die Idolatrie. Mit der Fotografie beginnt die ‚Nachgeschichte', und zwar als Kampf gegen die Textolatrie." Vilém Flusser: *Für eine Philosophie der Fotografie* (Göttingen: European Photography, 1983), 16.

3. „Die Jetztzeit, die als Modell der messianischen in einer ungeheuren Abbreviatur die Geschichte der ganzen Menschheit zusammenfasst, fällt haarscharf mit *der* Figur zusammen, die die Geschichte der Menschheit im Universum macht." Walter Benjamin: „Über den Begriff der Geschichte (1940)" in: *Gesammelte Schriften*, Band 1 (Frankfurt am Main: Suhrkamp, 1991), 703.

Aktualisierung von Vergangenheit adressiert wird; oder *Sputiamo su Hegel*[5] von Carla Lonzi, die den marxistischen Geschichtsbegriff aus feministischer Perspektive über seine Fundierung in der Hegelschen Dialektik angreift.[6]

4. „Poiché ovviamente il solo luogo in cui il passato può vivere è il presente, e se il presente non sente più il proprio passato come vivo, le università e i musei diventano luoghi problematici. E se l'arte e diventata oggi per noi una figura – forse *la* figura – eminente di questo passato, allora la domanda che occorre non stancarsi di porre è: qual è il luogo dell'arte nel presente?" Giorgio Agamben: *Creazione e anarchia. L'opera nell'età della religione capitalista* (Vicenza: Neri Pozza Editore, 2017), 10.

(Denn offensichtlich ist die Gegenwart der einzige Ort, an dem de Vergangenheit leben kann, und wenn die Gegenwart ihre eigene Vergangenheit nicht mehr als lebendig empfindet, werden Universitäten und Museen zu problematischen Orten. Und wenn die Kunst für uns heute zu einer herausragenden Figur – vielleicht *der* Figur – dieser Vergangenheit geworden ist, dann dürfen wir nicht müde werden, die Frage zu stellen: Welches ist der Ort der Kunst in der Gegenwart? Übers. d. Verf.)

5. „Esaminiamo il rapporto donna-uomo in Hegel, il filosofo che ha visto nel servo il momento traente della storia: egli, più insidiosamente di altri, ha razionalizzato il potere patriarcale nella dialettica tra un principio divino-femminile e un principio umano virile. Il primo presiede alla famiglia, il secondo alla comunità." Carla Lonzi: *Sputiamo su Hegel* (Milano: Scritti di Rivolta Femminile, 1977), 24–25.

(Untersuchen wir das Verhältnis zwischen Frau und Mann bei Hegel, dem Philosophen, der im Knecht das treibende Moment der Geschichte sah: Er rationalisierte, hinterhältiger als andere, die patriarchale Macht in der Dialektik zwischen einem göttlich-weiblichen Prinzip und einem humanen-männlichen Prinzip. Das erste herscht in der Familie, das zweite in der Gemeinschaft. (Übers. d. Verf.)

6. „In allen diesen Beziehungen ist und bleibt die Kunst nach der Seite ihrer höchsten Bestimmung für uns ein Vergangenes." Georg Wilhelm Friedrich Hegel: „Vorlesungen über die Ästhetik" in: *Werke in 20 Bänden und Register*, Band 13-1 (Frankfurt am Main: Suhrkamp, 2007), 25.

I

Der Film *Dopostoria* beginnt mit einem Farbfoto als Eingangsbild, dem einzigen übrigens, das ich selbst aufgenommen habe. Es zeigt den Blick vom Friedhof der Äolischen Insel Lipari hinüber auf die „Rocca Rossa", den roten Felsen am Meer mit seinen antiken Wehranlagen und dem archäologischen Museum darauf.[7] Das Foto bleibt jedoch nicht unverändert, sondern verwandelt sich langsam, wie im Entwicklerbad eines analogen Fotolabors: zuerst in sein eigenes Farbnegativ und dann weiter, bis es als Schwarz-Weiß-Negativ erscheint.

Die Geste der zweifachen Rückführung auf das eigene Negativ verweist auf den analogen fotografischen Prozess, bei dem das Originalnegativ letzte Zeugenschaft für den ursprünglichen fotografischen Akt ablegt.[8] Für jenen Moment also, in dem das fotografische Bild aus einer historischen Situation herausgeschnitten wurde, um es „festzuhalten" und fortan wieder hervorbringbar und verfügbar zu machen.[9] Die digitale, sich vor unserem Auge vollziehende Verwandlung des Bildes in sein eigenes Umkehrbild zeigt es an: Das analoge fotografische Original existiert nicht mehr, der mythische Akt der fotografischen Bildschöpfung ist an einen anderen Ort entschwunden.

7. Siehe das Bild auf dem Einband dieses Buches.

8. „The only 'objective' truth that photographs offer is the assertion that somebody or something [...] was somewhere and took a picture." Allan Sekula, *Photography Against the Grain* (Halifax: Press of Nova Scotia College of Art and Design, 1984), 57.

9. „[...] one can't possess the present but one can possess the past." Susan Sontag, *On Photography* (New York: Rosetta Books, 1977), 128.

In die Bildverarbeitungsprogramme vielleicht – aber vor allem in die mediale und soziale Distribution von Bildern.[10]

Maria Clara Martinelli, Archäologin am Museum in Lipari, spricht im ersten Kapitel des Films über die Bestattungskulturen seit der Zeit der Vorgeschichte. Die Verstorbenen wurden entweder verbrannt oder beerdigt. In den frühen Grabgefäßen aus Ton nehmen die Toten oft eine kniende Haltung ein. Die auswölbende Form der Gefäße verweist auf den Mutterbauch und damit auf die Verbindung von Tod und Geburt.[11] Das Filmbild bleibt hier schwarz, man hört nur die Stimme der Archäologin. Der Klang der Stimme ist es vor allem anderen, der ein Individuum ausmacht, der fragile Ausdruck seines Lebendigseins, welches sein späteres Verstummen bereits vorwegnimmt. Gegen Ende der Sequenz im Film spricht die Archäologin unvermittelt über die eigene Sterblichkeit.[12]

Das Nichtbild verstärkt die Körperlichkeit der Stimme. Es geht um etwas, das jenseits des Bildes liegt, jenseits jeder Vorstellung: um den Tod. Zuerst um den Tod der anderen, der sich in den Bestattungsritualen und im

10. „Die alte Magie ist vorgeschichtlich, sie ist älter als das historische Bewusstsein, die neue Magie ‚nachgeschichtlich', sie folgt auf das historische Bewusstsein. Die neue Zauberei sieht nicht darauf ab, die Welt da draußen, sondern unsere Begriffe betreffs der Welt zu verändern. Sie ist Magie zweiten Grades: abstraktes Gaukeln." Vilém Flusser: *Für eine Philosophie der Fotografie* (Göttingen: European Photography, 1983), 15–16.

11. Siehe den Beitrag von Maria Clara Martinelli ab S. 63 in diesem Band.

12. „Die Sagbarkeit ist an eine übergeordnete Instanz – die Stimme – als artikulierte Verlautbarung, *phone semantike*, gebunden. Aber zugleich ist der Stimme eine irreduzible Negativität eingeschrieben: die des Todes des Sprechenden und die Abwesenheit des in der Sprache Vermeinten." Julian Nida-Rümelin und Elif Özmen: *Philosophie der Gegenwart in Einzeldarstellungen* (Stuttgart: Kröner, 2. Auflage, 1999), 11.

Totenkult offenbart, welche zu den ältesten Formen menschlicher Kulturen gehören. Kultur heißt hier nichts anderes, als dass das Leben und Wirken der Mitglieder einer Gemeinschaft bewahrt und damit weiter genutzt werden können. So ist die Verbindung zwischen Tod und Geburt zu verstehen: Etwas wird weitergegeben. Die Grabgefäße, in denen die Toten in Embryostellungen fixiert sind, beziehen daher ihre Form: Sie sind bereit für die Wiedergeburt.

Der Tod selbst bleibt dabei im Dunkeln. Er ist das andere, nicht erreichbare Ufer. Ein Bild hat er nicht. Er ist mit der Kultur der Gemeinschaft verbunden. Ohne ein wie auch immer geartetes Eingehen des eigenen Lebens in die nachfolgenden Generationen gibt es kein Nachleben und damit keine Hoffnung.[13]

II

Die Bildsequenz des zweiten Kapitels beginnt mit der Pilgerkirche *San Lorenzo fuori le mura* und bewegt sich von dort weiter in den sich anschließenden Stadtfriedhof Roms, den *Cimitero Campo Verano,* eine wahrhafte Nekropole mit prachtvollen Alleen und mit Stadtvierteln der Toten verschiedener gesellschaftlicher Klassen und unterschiedlicher politischer sowie architektonischer Präferenzen, welche die lebendige Stadt Rom widerspiegeln. Hier geht es ganz im Sinne des römischen Barock um die Fassade, das Äußere – jedoch versetzt in die Zeit des italienischen Nationalstaates – und weniger um den intimen Inhalt der Gräber.

13. „Der Tod verbirgt kein Geheimnis. Er öffnet keine Tür. Er ist das Ende eines Menschen. Was von ihm überlebt, ist das, was er anderen Menschen gegeben hat, was in ihrer Erinnerung bleibt." Norbert Elias: *Über die Einsamkeit der Sterbenden in unseren Tagen* (Frankfurt am Main: Suhrkamp, 1982), 100.

Das Vokalstück von Carlo Gesualdo da Venosa, mit dem die Bildstrecke des modernen römischen Friedhofs unterlegt ist, stimmt auf eine ihr vorhergehende Zeit ein und gibt den Bildern der Gräber einen Bedeutungszusammenhang, der jenseits der Bildoberfläche liegt. Gesualdos Madrigal-Kompositionen sind durchdrungen von Schuld und Schmerz. Sie lassen die Harmonie der frühen Renaissancemusik hinter sich und kündigen bereits das Aufkommen des Barock an.

Während die Fotosequenz weiterläuft und einen Spaziergang auf einem menschenleeren Friedhof suggeriert, gibt sich das fotografische Material zunehmend als Archivbestand zu erkennen. Jedes Foto trägt rechts unten den gleichen Stempel. Teilweise sind die Kartons, auf die die Fotos montiert sind, mit ihren Beschriftungen zu sehen. Es wird also ein weiterer Zusammenhang eingeführt, der sich nicht mehr alleine auf den Kontext des sichtbaren Inhalts der Bilder bezieht, sondern auf den ihrer Archivierung.[14]

Fotoarchive sind mit dem Medium der analogen Fotografie eng verwandt. Malerei wird gesammelt, Fotografie dagegen wird archiviert, zunächst jedenfalls. Fotografien sind mächtige Zeugen einer entschwundenen Vergangenheit.[15] So entsteht im Film eine doppelte Verbindung zwischen dem Friedhof und dem Archiv sowie zwischen Fotografie

14. „The capacity for accurate description, the ability to establish distinct relations of time and event, image and statement, have come to define the terms of archival production proper to the language of those mechanical mediums, each of which give new phenomenological account of the world as image." Okwui Enwezor: *Archive Fever: Photography between History and the Monument* (New York: Steidl, 2007), 11–12.

15. „Having a photograph of Shakespeare would be like having a nail from the True Cross." Susan Sontag: *On Photography* (New York: Rosetta Books, 1977), 120.

und Tod. Der Friedhof als Abbild und zugleich als schweigender Gegenpol der Stadt Rom. Auch die Fotografien sind stumm – den abgebildeten Szenen wurde der Ton entzogen, jedes Mal beim Betrachten, immer wieder gerade eben: ein Verstummen.

Dann erscheint erneut ein Schwarzbild und dazu wieder eine Stimme, diesmal auf Deutsch. Sie gehört der Historikerin Carolin Kosuch, die über Bestattungskulturen der Moderne und hierbei über den langsamen Verfall des erdbestatteten Körpers im Vergleich zum „ausschleichenden" jüdischen Trauerritus spricht. Beides sind parallel verlaufende Prozesse hin zu einer zunehmenden Immaterialität des Todes.[16]

III

Das dritte und mittlere Kapitel ist das Kernstück des Films, zumal es sein Ausgangspunkt war. Es ging um die Frage, ob ein immenses kulturelles Gebilde wie das der Fotothek der Bibliotheca Hertziana in Rom in seiner Gesamtheit in einem Film abbildbar ist.

Ein solches Fotoarchiv ist ein Abgrund, oder mehr noch ein gigantisches Labyrinth, das sich nicht einfach überblicken und erfassen lässt. Wäre in einem hypothetischen Film jedes Bild der Fotothek nur jeweils eine Sekunde lang zu sehen, dann müsste dieser Film etwa zehn Tage und Nächte durchgehend laufen, bis alle Bilder des Archivs einmal erschienen wären. Obwohl die Einzelbilder dabei in den Hintergrund träten, würden im rhythmischen Fließen des fotografischen Bilderstroms Bildanalogien unterschwellig wahrnehmbar bleiben.

16. Siehe den Beitrag von Carolin Kosuch ab S. 51 in diesem Band.

Also habe ich zunächst eine individuelle Auswahl von Bildern aus dem Fotoarchiv der Hertziana getroffen, indem ich weder einer objektiven Methode noch dem Zufallsprinzip, sondern meinen eigenen Vorlieben und Interessen gefolgt bin. Suchbegriffe zu architektonischen Monumenten in Rom wie zum Beispiel „Obelisco", „Mausoleo" oder auch zu Mussolinis „Foro Italico" ergaben jeweils eine erste Auswahl von Fotografien für thematische Bildgruppen mit visuellen und inhaltlichen Verbindungen.

Dann habe ich die Bilder als Filmsequenzen derart montiert, dass jedes einzelne Foto jeweils einmal mit dem vorhergehenden und einmal mit dem darauffolgenden Bild überlagert wird – also AB, BC, CD, DE, EF etc. Im Film entsteht durch die rasche Abfolge der Bilder innerhalb einer thematischen Gruppe von Fotografien so eine Art „Abdruck" des Archivs, welcher von den Fähigkeiten des Publikums profitiert, Bildsequenzen schnell zu einem Gesamteindruck verschiedener Bildtypologien zusammenfassen zu können. Es ist eine rasante, circa siebenminütige phantasmagorische Reisestrecke durch Rom und gleichzeitig durch verschiedene Teilgebiete, „Provinzen" der Fotothek.

DAS ANDERE DES ARCHIVS

Für ein Archiv gilt dasselbe wie für die Fotografie, dass es – jedenfalls als Ganzes – stumm bleibt.

Wie kann man einem Archiv eine Stimme verleihen oder einen Klang? Dafür bedarf es zunächst eines Publikums, eines Gegenübers. Letztendlich ist dies eine Frage nach den mit dem Archiv verbundenen Körpern sowie auch nach dem Körper des Archivs selbst.

Ich wollte die Geschichte aus ihrer Erstarrung lösen, in Bewegung versetzen, rhythmisieren. Das bedeutete, das Archiv, in das bestimmte Geschichtsbilder eingeschrieben sind, zum Gegenstand, zum künstlerischen Material zu machen und dabei zu transformieren.[17] Dieser Transformationsprozess erforderte es aber, weder die Kontinuität des Alten im Neuen zuzulassen noch eine kategorische Opposition zum Bestehenden einzunehmen, wodurch das Alte ebenfalls bestätigt würde. Stattdessen sollte, wie ein Gespenst, jenes abwesende Andere des Archivs aufscheinen können.[18] Es muss nur für kurze Momente kontrastierend wahrnehmbar sein, um das Archiv als das sichtbar werden zu lassen, was es tatsächlich ist: ein wirkmächtiges Netzwerk von Bildern und Beziehungen.

Das Archiv selbst bleibt dabei abstrakt, was bedeutet, dass es noch immer keinen eigenen Körper hat.[19] Letztlich sollte es aber weniger um eine konkrete Serie von Bildern

17. „[. . .] man muss diese versteinerten Verhältnisse dadurch zum Tanzen zwingen, dass man ihnen ihre eigne Melodie vorsingt!" Karl Marx: *Zur Kritik der Hegelschen Rechtsphilosophie* (Paris: Deutsch-Französische Jahrbücher, 1844), 74.

18. „Gibt es nicht vielleicht auch eine *Zeit für Gespenster*, eine *Phantomzeit*, eine Wiederkehr der Bilder, ein ‚Nachleben', die nicht dem Übertragungsmodell einer Nachahmung der antiken Werke durch jüngere unterworfen wäre? Gibt es nicht vielleicht auch eine *Zeit für die Erinnerung* an Bilder, ein dunkles Spiel des Verdrängten und seiner ewigen Wiederkehr, eine andere Zeit als die von dieser Kunstgeschichte, dieser Darstellung vorgeschlagene?" Georges Didi-Huberman: *Das Nachleben der Bilder. Kunstgeschichte und Phantomzeit nach Aby Warburg*; aus dem Französischen von Michael Bischoff (Berlin: Suhrkamp, 2010), 29.

19. „In structural terms, the archive is both an abstract paradigmatic entity and a concrete institution. In both senses, the archive is a vast substitution set, providing for a relation of general equivalence between images." Allan Sekula: „The Body and the Archive" in: *October 39* (Cambridge: MIT Press, 1986), 17.

noch um ein einzelnes Archiv gehen, sondern mehr um ein System, für welches dieses Archiv ein Symptom darstellt.

Geschichtsauffassungen können nicht aus sich selbst heraus transformiert werden, sondern müssen radikal anders dargestellt werden.[20] Archive sind nie neutral, sondern tendieren zur Selbsterhaltung. Darin besteht die Herausforderung für ihre künstlerische Bearbeitung. Wer die Regeln des Archivs akzeptiert, ist schon verloren oder besser gesagt kann sich seiner Vorannahmen nicht mehr entziehen. Das ist die Logik des Archivs.

Bei der Fotothek der Bibliotheca Hertziana, die mit einem Bestand von mehr als 870.000 Aufnahmen – vornehmlich zur italienischen Kunst und Architektur von der Spätantike bis in die Gegenwart – zu den führenden kunsthistorischen Fotoarchiven weltweit gehört, handelt es sich streng genommen nicht um ein Archiv, sondern um eine *museale Sammlung*, denn die darin als Fotos verwahrten Kunstwerke werden durch ihre Aufnahme in die Fotothek von der Institution als kunstgeschichtlich relevant nobilitiert. Was umgekehrt bedeutet, dass der gesamte Rest, also all jenes *Andere* einer Kunstrichtung bzw. eines Zeitabschnitts, sich außerhalb der Sammlung und damit jenseits eines kunstgeschichtlichen Kanons wiederfindet, der von der Institution vorgegeben wurde.[21]

20. Audre Lorde: „The Master's Tools Will Never Dismantle the Master's House," in: *Sister Outsider* (Berkeley: Crossing Press, 1984), 110–113.

21. „The West would therefore remain unable […] to conceive of an Other to what it calls human – an Other, therefore, to its correlated postulates of power, truth, freedom. All other modes of being human would instead have to be seen not as the alternative modes of being human that they are 'out there,' but adaptively, as the lack of the West's ontologically absolute self-description." Sylvia Wynter: „Unsettling the Coloniality of Being/Power/Truth/Freedom Towards the Human, After Man, Its Overrepresentation—An Argument," *CR: The New Centennial Review 3*, Nr. 3 (2003), 282.

Also blieb nur der Bruch mit den vorgegebenen Benutzungsordnungen des Archivs, um eine künstlerische Perspektive auf die darin präsentierten Geschichten einnehmen zu können, um aus dem Archiv heraus jenes abwesende Andere aufzurufen und dabei nichtsdestotrotz für sich in Anspruch zu nehmen, einen künstlerischen Zugang zu dem Archiv als Ganzem zu schaffen, indem das Archiv selbst in einer quasi-zeremoniellen Geste aus der Gegenwart heraus in die Vergangenheitsform verwandelt und derart transformiert wieder in die Welt entlassen wird: Dopostoria.

Die Bildsequenz des dritten Kapitels ist mit dem Auszug einer Klavierkomposition von Julius Eastman für mehrere Flügel unterlegt.[22] Die Verbindung von Eastmans Musik mit den kanonischen Bildern einer europäischen Kunstgeschichte setzt einen notwendigen Kontrapunkt zu dem Fotoarchiv des über hundert Jahre alten, renommierten Instituts zur Erforschung der italienischen Kunst in Rom, das sich in seiner Geschichte hauptsächlich auf eine weiße, exklusiv europäische Perspektive der Kunstgeschichte beschränkt hat. Diese hat die für sie konstitutiven Bedingungen dessen, was sie ausschließt – wie Ausgrenzung, Ausbeutung, Sklaverei und Kolonialismus –, lange Zeit ausgeblendet. Eastmans Musik wird in dieser Filmsequenz gleichsam als jenes konkrete „Andere" dem Archiv gegenübergestellt, ohne dessen eigene Kontexte noch einmal zu thematisieren.[23] Sie trägt aber dazu bei, jenes in der Kunstgeschichte Verdrängte bzw. sein nunmehr offensichtlich gewordenes Fehlen aufzurufen.[24]

22. Siehe auch die „audiovisuelle Komposition" *The Third Part of the Third Measure* (2017) des Künstlerkollektivs *The Otolith Group* (Anjalika Sagar und Kodwo Eshun), die Julius Eastmans politisches und kompositorisches Werk künstlerisch reinszeniert. http://otolithgroup.org.

So wie die im Film eingesetzten Bildsequenzen durch ihre Rhythmen, Pausen und Widerstände zeitliche Ausdrucksformen einer Bildsprache sind, arbeiten auch die musikalischen Stücke sowohl mit als auch gegen die Logik des Archivs, als verbindende Elemente und als Distanzierungen zugleich.

IV

Im vierten Kapitel wird in kurzen Zwischentiteln auf schwarzem Grund eine Geschichte erzählt. Wieder steht eine Stimme bzw. ihre Abwesenheit und ihr Wiedererscheinen als „innere Stimme" beim Lesen der Untertitel im Zentrum. Formal knüpft das vierte Kapitel damit an meinen früheren Film *Anarcheology* an, zu dem *Dopostoria* Bezüge hat. Die persönliche Geschichte handelt von der Fragilität des Lebens und beginnt mit einem Traum.

23. „There is need to read Eastman's work not only within its musical sensitivity, structure or texture – (ar)rhythmic, (dis)harmony, phonic – but also consider Eastman as a political being who saw his work as a medium to deliberate on the sociopolitical, economy, religion, as well as issues of gender, race and sexuality. While race and sexuality were very important and played a primal role in Eastman's compositions, they were not the only topics Eastman dealt with, which is the impression one gets when one peruses articles and narrations about Eastman today. Especially with the rhetoric of the 'rediscovery' of Eastman within the music and visual art fields, which in itself sounds like giving light to darkness, Eastman is particularly portrayed – if not reduced – to his blackness and his gayness." Bonaventure Soh Bejeng Ndikung, „I Love to Love, Oh Pleasant Love. The Marvel of Julius Eastman", https://www.arsenal-berlin.de/en/berlinale-forum/archive/program-archive/2018/magazine/articles/the-marvel-of-julius-eastman/.

24. „Wollen wir die Repräsentationen und das Ungedachte, die aus dieser Vergangenheit [der Kolonialzeit] resultieren, hinter uns lassen, bedarf es der Arbeit an der Geschichte und an der Vorstellungswelt eines Verhältnisses, das selbst noch der Dekolonisierung harrt." Felwine Sarr und Benedicte Savoy: *Zurückgeben. Über die Restitution afrikanischer Kulturgüter* (Berlin: Matthes & Seitz, 2019), 76–77.

CAROLIN KOSUCH: ON BURIAL CULTURES IN MODERNITY*

Let me tell you a little about Jacob Moleschott, who was one of the most famous materialists—a natural scientist, physiologist, and doctor from the Netherlands. He taught in Heidelberg for a long time but was expelled from the university because of his anti-clerical, anti-Christian ideas. He was then taken in by the kingdom of Italy, where he was appointed senator and given a laboratory in Turin. He spoke out in favor of cremation in his book *Cycle of Life* (*Kreislauf des Lebens*, 1852), one of the most famous texts of scientific materialism from the nineteenth century. However, I think that as a natural scientist influenced by Protestantism, he looked at the body—at corporeality, death, and dying—differently than the Catholics of Italy. With him, we do not find the idea of preserving the ashes of the dead or any related sentiments for the aftercare of human remains. On the contrary, he advocated getting rid of cemeteries and scattering the ashes of the dead so that the matter they were made of could quickly be used as fertilizer in the fields. He envisioned making the dead useful for the living in this way. And that idea of utilization naturally leads us right back to the twentieth century.

Indeed, this was especially the case with Protestant cremationists. For the Catholics in Italy, it was primarily a matter of classifying the dead in the national *memoria* and separating them from nature and its cycles. But the cremationists wanted to take them further in the direction of progress, modernity, and technology.

The question of space was fundamental and essentially at the root of this whole debate. Cremationists ultimately

*This text is based on the transcript of a research interview.

wanted the nation to prosper—this was the nineteenth century, when national movements and patriotism abounded. Against the backdrop of the progressive and the modern, nineteenth century cremationists assumed that the population would continue to grow, and it no longer seemed legitimate to concede the dead that much space. That is why they wanted to incinerate them—to reduce them to the solid elements from which they were built. Jakob Moleschott, for example, was fascinated by the role of phosphorous. I examined his lab diary at the archive in Bologna; it gives you a good impression of the experiments he conducted to find out where phosphorus is needed in the body in the first place. He discovered that phosphorus is important for the brain and reasoned that the more phosphorus is in the brain, the bigger the brain and the more powerful a human being's thoughts. Moleschott thought that this substance would contribute to the world progressing, to enlightenment and intelligence progressing. And where was phosphorus stored? In his opinion: in the dead. He concluded that they should be cremated quickly so that the phosphorus would be released and then reused to ensure the nation's progress. Given this imagined prosperity, space was clearly an important issue.

In my opinion, one has to look at the reasoning behind the arguments used by these nationalist movements. Especially in Italy, but also in Germany, one finds that some of the very radical patriots wanted to distance themselves from the Christian heritage. In the sense of an "invention of tradition," they sought grounds to legitimize their nationhood. To do this, these patriots looked back to pre-Christian times: the Italians looked to the ancient Romans, Greeks, and Egyptians, and the Germans to ancient Germanic peoples. The linguist and mythologist Jakob Grimm was one of the first to publicly advocate cremation in the German-speaking world. There is a text based on a lecture from 1849 in which he exalts the so-called "barbaric" Germanic peoples and imagines the custom of cremation as a wild, free, and liberating tradition. He positions it against the slow decomposition in the soil associated with Christianity. Archaeology played a significant role in this and archaeological finds were repeatedly used to legitimize cremation.

Ultimately, it was also about not excluding the body of the dead citizen from the nation but integrating it—albeit only after it had been rendered "harmless." The cremated body can no longer spread diseases because it no longer decomposes—a point repeatedly emphasized by the cremationists of the nineteenth century. They both borrowed from and also contributed to an important discourse of the time, namely of hygiene. It raised the idea that when the dead decomposed, contagious substances would be released into the cemetery's water and soil, threatening the living. Epidemics like cholera and typhoid were traced back to such mechanisms. Cremationists looked to Paris and London, where cases of overcrowded cemeteries had been reported before the cemetery reforms of the nineteenth century. As you probably know, before the nineteenth century, Christian churchyards were located within the cities. Therefore in times of great epidemics, those places of the dead stood in danger of becoming overpopulated. There were reports of graves collapsing and the pressure causing corpses to push into the wine cellars of nearby homes. Of course, people found that to be disgusting and revolting. Such concepts were current at that time: disgust, repulsion, loathing for the dead.

In order to address that in a civilizing way, cremationists aimed to render the dead body "harmless" through cremation. But the dead human being also became part of a history—the history of modernity, because, as ashes, it could theoretically no longer decay. The ashes are what remain. Some architects around that time designed crematoria with columbaria for the urns, so that the material remains of the dead would remain part of the nation—according to the prevailing logic of the time—instead of being buried or scattered. There were even ideas from revolutionary France, around 1789, that the ashes of the dead could be processed into glass, which would then be used as construction material for buildings, urn halls, and crematoria. So what it was really about was keeping the dead in history, in the history of modernity.

My view is that we can use burial culture, and how the dead are dealt with, as a lens to examine the historical developments of an era. I do not think about the cremations as a singular phenomenon but use their history to grasp the imaginary world of a particular group leading a powerful discourse at that time. Ultimately, such imaginaries are especially palpable in liminal phenomena such as death and dying. I have done a lot of research into Jewish history, which has shaped my view of historical phenomena. The Jews are a particular phenomenon in history: they are a small group living within a much larger community, which in Europe is a Christian community. Whenever you look at such minorities that do not belong to the "norm," so to speak, I think you can see much deeper into history and gain completely new insights. You can study the historical role of emperors and kings, who are at the center of power and influence. But what happens further away can be seen particularly well at the margins, in groups that have been marginalized in the historical process, such as Jews and women. Upheavals and threshold moments are legible in their particular histories. Death, too, is one such history at the margins. There is a lot to learn from such histories within history.

The period of mourning is stipulated by the laws and the approaches specific to memorial culture, including the mourning rites. According to Jewish tradition, the bereaved should go back to normal life after up to one year. As an immediate relative, at the beginning of the mourning period, you are not supposed to change clothes, leave the house, and so on. The mourning process occurs in phases, with the main mourning periods being *shiva* and *sheloshim,* and, depending on your relationship to the deceased, ending after a year. Think of it as a successive dilution of mourning. That is how religions absorb death and mourning. Christianity also has similar anniversaries of remembrance such as the Sunday of the Dead and All Souls Day. With regard to the pyramids, it is worth adding that the first models of crematoria date to the time of the French Revolution. Pierre Giraud came up with a model of what such an oven and columbarium could look like: a big pyramid with an incinerator inside, which he imagined enclosed by a grove for the urns, or a columbarium where the ashes of the dead would be kept. There you have a pyramid again: it is clearly a recurring motif. Of course, it is also due to the Egyptomania of the time, as people sought the exotic and foreign in places other than their own; and Egyptian culture was indeed associated with death and dying.

In principle, it is about commemorative culture. One of the most prominent Italian cremationists, Paolo Gorini, who also designed a crematorium, makes a distinction here: For him, the dead who were important to the nation, like Giuseppe Mazzini, were not to be cremated but preserved. Such great national figures were to be shown to the population in traveling exhibitions. This was also about strengthening national sentiment. But even preserved bodies were subject to temporality: they were to be cremated as soon as they lost their significance to the community.

There is the idea of the Christian cemetery—which brings us back to the question of space—as an exempt space, that is, a special space connecting the dead and the living. It is the place of the dead to which the living can come again and again. And this place was connected to the Christian churches. The dead and the living both belonged to the *Christianitas*, the whole of Christendom. For the cremationists it was hard to propose something different to compete with this. There was no secular place to guarantee this form of—and here comes an important word—"holiness." And this sense of loss—which can be found in the primary literature of letters, newspaper reports, and debates around cremation—is something they were very aware of at that time: that the nation, with all its patriotism, aesthetics, and honor for the dead, could ultimately not compensate for religious transcendence or spiritual holiness. There was a void. But that is where technology came in, and the discourse of progress, with materiality and the materialism of the natural sciences: namely, the idea that the material of the dead is taken back into the cycle of nature, and that the dead are not really dead but transformed into new life. It was about acceleration—and here we have another moment of modernity, modernity as a moment of unbelievable acceleration, not only with regard to the railway or postal traffic, or migration from the country to the city, but also with regard to the dead. The dead no longer lie statically in the cemetery; the dead move and indeed return to life in a new form.

Perhaps one can generally say that in monotheistic religions, cremation was thought of as a punishment and was therefore not considered legitimate. Judaism buries the dead; Christianity followed suit. Islam also buries the dead. The Germanic tribes sometimes incinerated their dead. In India, burning the bodies of the deceased remains a custom to this day. The ancient Romans sometimes burned their dead, but there is also evidence of earth burials. Because the Roman Empire was a religiously and socially diverse territory, a variety of burial forms could be found there. Interestingly enough, the modern cremationists of the nineteenth century referred back to ancient Rome, the Greeks, the Germanic tribes, and the Indians, imagining cremation as an original custom that was merely ousted by Christianity. Cremation had already been banned by Charlemagne in the early Middle Ages, and if you look at history, heretics and heretical books were burnt. So this was also a form of purification in the spiritual sense. Those believed to threaten the Christian faith were burnt at the stake. And this carried over into the material sphere in the nineteenth century. While witch burnings took place in early modern Europe, the modern era had microbial purity in mind, no longer spiritual purity. It is quite interesting. This marked the shift from pre-modernity to modernity. Of course, the whole scientific discourse was connected to this, as microscopes were invented and used to discover the micro-world. The question arose: Where do these diseases actually come from? For a long time, the miasma theory prevailed: the idea that harmful fumes caused diseases. At some point, it was discovered that there were small material bodies, called corpuscles, and then bacteria were discovered. This was the beginning of the modern hygiene discourse about microbial purity, strengthening the defense system, and the healthy body in a healthy state. It was all politicized and culturally influenced.

The cremationists, meanwhile, saw the earth as a slow element, connected with the feminine, but also with the clergy—in other words, with everything that was condemned as premodern in this secularist discourse. The earth was interpreted as slow, decaying, evaporating, opaque, oppressive, and constraining. This idea was also transferred to the womb, which symbolized the dark confinement from which new human beings were to free themselves and progress toward the light. In cremation discourse, this was contrasted with the fast, accelerating, male-coded element. So, the cremation discourse of the nineteenth century juxtaposed male and female codings, which were also linked to the elements. In the religious context, the dominant idea was that the dead were released into the ground, into the earth of the fathers. With cremation, this was reversed. That idea also plays a role in my book: that the gender discourse of the nineteenth century, as it were, extends to death through the idea of cremation.

This has a lot to do with movement and the spatial dimension. When the dead body is lowered into the earth and decays there, the body is still materially present for quite a while. It is actually similar to *shiva* and *sheloshim,* and the gradual dilution we spoke about earlier, but with the decay of the dead body: first, it is still there materially, and then it continues to decay. Whereas if you put an urn into the ground, or don't put it into the ground but in a columbarium, the end product is already there. It does not change any further. In this respect—and this is also a contemporary discourse—the slow decomposition in the earth is a process that is closer to human beings and nature, which corresponds to our emotions and feelings of mourning. We are particularly affected at the beginning, and the more that time passes, the more we are perhaps absorbed by everyday life again—this is a rhythm that is perhaps connoted with premodernity. At this point, we could address Günter Anders by asking: Is humanity antiquated? Are we overtaking ourselves with our technology, our mechanization, which no longer corresponds to our own rhythm? The nineteenth century was already dealing with such questions. Namely, with which emotions one encounters the grave, and with which one encounters the urn—there is a difference. In the case of the urn, as the writings of the time make clear, one tends to be distanced and dignified but no longer emotionally affected, whereas the emotions at the graveside are more present. At the time, many people wanted to leave strong emotions behind; they saw themselves as progressive and enlightened, not excessive and uncontrollably emotional, which they associated with the image of mourning women.

The first German crematorium that was actually used was built by Friedrich Siemens. And it was also widely advertised, for example, in the bourgeois family magazine *Gartenlaube*. There is a picture of a Protestant priest blessing the coffin, which is no longer lowered into the ground but into an incineration chamber, so that the moment of lowering, of saying goodbye, is essentially copied, but it moves toward technology instead of slow decomposition in the ground. And it was considered unaesthetic, even inadmissible, that after this blessing, this farewell, helpers should touch the coffin again in the cremation room, before the cremation. So Siemens devised a mechanism that bridged this moment of uncertainty. Ultimately, technology is what bridged the uncertainty of how to deal with the dead, after the farewell but before the cremation in the crematorium. The coffin was lowered and transported into the oven by a system of rollers so that no human hand would touch it anymore; only the ashes, which are, after all, a product, a manufactured product, would eventually be collected by human hands and put into the urn. And that makes perfect sense to me: that there was obviously a debate about that, and that the cremationists had felt inhibited. I think that this way of dealing with touch reveals a lot about how the secular cremationists dealt with death.

CAROLIN KOSUCH: ÜBER BESTATTUNGSKULTUREN IN DER MODERNE*

Ich erzähle Ihnen ein bisschen was über Jakob Moleschott, der einer der bekanntesten Materialisten war, Naturwissenschaftler, Physiologe und Arzt aus den Niederlanden. Er hat lange Zeit in Heidelberg gelehrt und wurde dann wegen seiner antiklerikalen, antichristlichen Haltung relegiert und fand im Königreich Italien Aufnahme. Dort wurde er zum Senator ernannt und hat auch ein Labor in Turin eingerichtet bekommen. Und er hat sich in seinem *Kreislauf des Lebens*, das ist eine der bekanntesten naturwissenschaftlich-materialistischen Schriften des 19. Jahrhunderts, für die Feuerbestattung ausgesprochen. Allerdings, und das ist ganz interessant, blickt er als protestantisch geprägter Naturwissenschaftler, so glaube ich, auf Körper, Körperlichkeit, Tod und Sterben, anders als die Katholiken Italiens. Bei ihm finden wir nicht die Vorstellung, die Asche der Toten zu konservieren, auch keinen vergleichbaren Nachsorge-Gedanken. Im Gegenteil plädiert er dafür, die Friedhöfe aufzulösen, die Asche der Toten zu verstreuen, sodass man die Materie, aus denen sie bestanden, schnell wieder nutzen kann, um die Äcker fruchtbar zu machen. So hatte er sich vorgestellt, die Toten für die Lebenden nutzbar zu machen. Und da sind wir natürlich ganz schnell wieder im 20. Jahrhundert, bei diesem Verwertungsgedanken.

Ja, und das findet sich eben verstärkt bei den protestantischen Feuerbestattern. Bei den katholischen hier in Italien geht es primär erstmal darum, die Toten in die nationale Memoria einzuordnen und sie von der Natur und ihren

*Dieser Text basiert auf der Abschrift eines Forschungsinterviews.

Kreisläufen zu separieren. Sie sollten in Richtung Fortschritt, in Richtung Moderne, in Richtung Technik mitgenommen werden, so die vorherrschende Ansicht der Feuerbestatter.

Die Raumfrage ist grundlegend oder liegt sozusagen am Beginn dieser ganzen Debatte. Denn es geht diesen Zeitgenossen letztlich darum, dass die Nation prosperiert, wir bewegen uns ja im Zeitraum des 19. Jahrhunderts, Nationalbewegungen und Patriotismus prosperieren. Vor dem Horizont des Progressiven, des Modernen gehen die Feuerbestatter des 19. Jahrhunderts davon aus, dass die Bevölkerung weiter anwächst, ihnen scheint es nicht mehr legitim, den Toten zu viel Platz einzuräumen. Und deshalb wollen sie sie veraschen. Sie reduzieren sie auf die festen Elemente, aus denen sie aufgebaut sind. Jakob Moleschott, von dem ich gerade sprach, macht zum Beispiel das Phosphor ganz stark. Ich habe sein Labor-Tagebuch in Bologna im Archiv ausgewertet. Da kann man sehr schön nachvollziehen, welche Experimente er machte, um herauszufinden, wo Phosphor im Körper überhaupt benötigt wird. Und er findet also heraus, Phosphor ist wichtig für das Gehirn. Und nun zieht er den Schluss, je mehr Phosphor im Gehirn ist, umso größer wird das Gehirn, umso gedankenstärker wird der Mensch. Letztlich trägt dieser Stoff in seiner Deutung also dazu bei, dass die Welt voranschreitet, die Aufklärung schreitet voran, die Intelligenz schreitet voran. Und wo ist Phosphor gespeichert? Seiner Meinung nach in den Toten. Deshalb müssen sie in seiner Logik schnell verbrannt werden, damit das Phosphor freigesetzt wird, sodass es sozusagen wieder verwendet wird, um den Fortschritt der Nation zu sichern. Und angesichts dieser vorgestellten Prosperität ist Raum natürlich eine wichtige Frage, klar.

Meiner Meinung nach muss man die Begründungszusammenhänge betrachten, die diese Nationalbewegten für ihre Argumentation heranziehen. Und gerade im italienischen, aber auch im deutschen Fall ist es so, dass einige der ganz radikalen Patrioten sich vom christlichen Erbe abgrenzen wollen. Sie verfolgen im Sinne einer *Invention of Tradition* die Frage, woher eigentlich die Legitimationsgründe für das eigene Nation-Sein kommen sollen. Hierzu greifen diese Patrioten in eine vorchristliche Zeit zurück, in Italien entsprechend in die römische Zeit, in die griechische Zeit, auch die ägyptische Zeit. Und im deutschen Fall auf die germanische Zeit. Einer der ersten, der die Feuerbestattung im deutschsprachigen Raum publik gemacht hat, ist der Sprach- und Mythenforscher Jakob Grimm. Es gibt eine Schrift, basierend auf einem Vortrag von 1849, in dem er die sogenannten barbarischen germanischen Völker hochleben lässt und den Brauch der Feuerbestattung als eine wilde, freie, befreiende Tradition imaginiert. Sie positioniert er gegen das langsame, mit dem Christlichen in Verbindung gebrachte Verwesen in der Erde. Dabei spielt Archäologie eine ganz große Rolle. Archäologische Funde werden als Legimitationsgrund für die Feuerbestattungen immer wieder herangezogen.

Letztlich geht es auch darum, den Körper des toten Bürgers nicht aus der Nation auszuschließen, sondern ihn zu integrieren. Allerdings nur in einer „unschädlich" gemachten Form. Der verbrannte Körper kann keine Krankheiten mehr verbreiten, weil er nicht mehr verwest. Das betonen die Feuerbestatter des 19. Jahrhunderts immer wieder. Sie lehnen sich an einen bedeutenden Diskurs der Zeit an und befördern ihn zugleich: jenen der Hygiene. Darin existiert die Vorstellung, dass beim Zerfall der Toten über Wasser und Erde des Friedhofes Krankheitsstoffe frei werden, die die Lebenden bedrohen, weil Epidemien wie

Cholera oder Typhus auf solche Mechanismen zurückgehen. Und die Feuerbestatter schauen nach Paris und London, von dort wurden einzelne Fälle einer Überbelegung von Friedhöfen in der Zeit vor der Friedhofsreform des 19. Jahrhunderts berichtet. Sie wissen ja, vor dem 19. Jahrhundert lagen die christlichen Kirchhöfe innerhalb der Städte. Und in Zeiten von großen Epidemien drohten diese Stätten der Toten, überfüllt zu werden. Es gibt also Berichte darüber, dass einzelne Gräber aufbrachen und die Toten sich in Weinkeller benachbarter Häuser hineindrückten. Und das ist für die Zeitgenossen natürlich eine eklige Vorstellung, eine widerliche Vorstellung. Das sind auch Begriffe dieser Zeit: Ekel, Widerwärtigkeit, Abscheu den Toten gegenüber. Und um das sozusagen zivilisatorisch aufzufangen, machen die Feuerbestatter den toten Körper durch die Einäscherung in diesem Sinn letztlich „unschädlich". Der tote Mensch wird aber auch zum Teil einer Geschichte, nämlich der Geschichte der Moderne, weil er in Form der Asche ja theoretisch nicht mehr verfallen kann. Die Asche ist das, was bleibt. Es gibt zeitgenössische Entwürfe von Architekten, von Krematorien mit Kolumbarien, in denen die Urnen aufgestellt sind, sodass der materielle Rest dieser Toten in der Logik dieser Zeit Teil der Nation bleibt und eben nicht vergraben oder verstreut wird. Und es gibt sogar Ideen, die kommen aus dem revolutionären Frankreich um 1789, dass man die Asche der Toten nutzt, um Glas zu pressen, und dieses Glas als Baustoffe verwendet für Gebäude, für Urnenhallen, für Krematorien. Es geht diesen Menschen also tatsächlich darum, die Toten in der Geschichte zu halten, in der Geschichte der Moderne.

Mein Blick geht eher dahin zu sagen, dass man über die Bestattungskultur, über die Art und Weise, wie mit den Toten umgegangen wird, wie in einem Brennglas

Entwicklungen der Zeit bündeln kann. Ich schaue mir die Feuerbestattungen nicht als eigenes Phänomen an, sondern ich nutze ihre Geschichte, um letztlich die Vorstellungswelt einer bestimmten, diskursmächtigen Gruppe einzufangen. Und solche Vorstellungen kann man an den letzten Dingen als Grenzphänomene, an Tod und Sterben ganz besonders gut festmachen. Ich habe viel zur jüdischen Geschichte gearbeitet. Das hat meinen Blick auf historische Phänomene geprägt, denn die Juden als historische Akteure sind auch ein Partikularphänomen, sie sind eine kleine Gruppe, die in einer jeweils viel viel größeren Gemeinschaft lebt – in Europa in einer christlichen. Und immer wenn man sich solche Minderheiten ansieht, die sozusagen nicht zur Norm gehören, glaube ich, kann man viel tiefer in die Geschichte blicken und ganz neue Erkenntnisse gewinnen. Sie können Kaiser und Könige in ihrer Geschichtlichkeit studieren, bei denen Macht und Einfluss zentriert sind, aber was weiter passiert, kann man ganz besonders an den Rändern absehen, bei im historischen Prozess marginalisierten Gruppen, etwa Juden und Jüdinnen, auch Frauen. In ihren Geschichten lassen sich Umbrüche, Schwellenmomente ablesen. Auch der Tod ist so eine Geschichte am Rande. Von solchen Geschichten in der Geschichte kann man viel lernen.

Für den zeitlichen Ablauf sorgt ja sozusagen das Gesetz und die Art des Umgangs mit der Memorialkultur, auch der Trauerritus. Wobei die jüdische Tradition spätestens nach einem Jahr die Hinterbliebenen wieder ins Leben entlässt. Als Trauernder oder als direkter Hinterbliebener darf man ja zunächst die Kleider nicht wechseln, das Haus nicht verlassen usw. Der Trauerprozess ist nach Shiva und Sheloshim, den eigentlichen Trauerzeiten, gestaffelt; spätestens aber nach einem Jahr endet er ganz. Das kann man sich wie eine sukzessive Verdünnung von Trauer vorstellen. So fangen die Religionen Tod und Trauer auf. Das Christentum hat ja ähnliche Jahrestage des Gedenkens, etwa den Totensonntag. Im Hinblick auf die Pyramiden wollte ich noch anführen, dass es erste Modelle von Krematorien aus der Zeit der Französischen Revolution gibt, die Pierre Giraud entworfen hat. Er hat also ein Modell entworfen, wie so ein Ofen und ein Kolumbarium aussehen könnte. Und was macht er? Er hat eine große Pyramide entworfen und darin ist der Verbrennungsofen untergebracht. Ringsum stellte er sich einen Urnenhain oder einen Urnengang vor, in dem die Asche der Toten aufbewahrt wird. Da haben Sie wieder Ihre Pyramide, das ist ganz klar so ein Motiv, das immer wieder auftaucht. Das ist natürlich auch der Ägyptomanie der Zeit geschuldet, mit der man das exotische Fremde an anderen Orten als dem eigenen suchte, und auch der Tatsache, dass man die ägyptische Kultur mit dem Tod und dem Sterben in Verbindung gebracht hat.

Einer der bedeutendsten italienischen Feuerbestatter und Erbauer eines Krematoriums, Paolo Gorini, differenziert an dieser Stelle. Seiner Ansicht nach sollen die Toten, die wichtig für die Nation sind, etwas Giuseppe Mazzini, nicht verbrannt, sondern konserviert werden. In Wanderausstellungen sollen diese Großen der Nation der Bevölkerung gezeigt werden. Hier geht es auch um eine Stärkung des Nationalgefühls. Allerdings unterliegen auch deren konservierte Körper einer Zeitlichkeit: Sie werden kremiert, sobald sie ihre Bedeutung für die Gemeinschaft verloren haben.

Es gibt ja die Vorstellung des christlichen Friedhofes, da sind wir wieder beim Raum als einem exemten Raum, also einem besonderen Raum, der die Toten und die Lebenden verbindet. Das ist der Ort der Toten, zu dem die Lebenden immer wieder kommen können. Dieser Ort ist aber mit den christlichen Kirchen verbunden. Tote und Lebende gehören zur Christianitas, zur Ganzheit. Und dem können die Feuerbestatter eigentlich nichts entgegensetzen. Es gibt keinen säkularen Ort, der diese Form von – und jetzt kommt ein wichtiges Wort, nämlich „Heiligkeit" – garantieren könnte. Und dieses Verlustgefühl, das finden wir in den Quellen, wenn ich mir Briefe anschaue, wenn ich mir Zeitungsberichte anschaue, Debatten rund um die Feuerbestattung, ist den Zeitgenossen sehr wohl bewusst, dass sozusagen die Nation, das patriotische Gefühl, das Gefühl von Ästhetik, auch von Ehre den Toten gegenüber, dass das eine religiöse Transzendenz oder eine spirituelle Heiligkeit letztlich nicht auffangen oder kompensieren kann. Da ist eine Leerstelle. Und an diese Stelle rückt die Technik, an diese Stelle rückt auch der Diskurs von Fortschritt, das Materielle oder der naturwissenschaftliche Materialismus, nämlich die Vorstellung, dass das Material der Toten wieder in den Kreislauf der Natur aufgenommen wird, dass die Toten also nicht wirklich tot sind, sondern wieder in neues Leben transformiert werden. Da geht es um Beschleunigung, da haben wir wieder einen Moment der Moderne, die Moderne als Moment der unglaublichen Beschleunigung, nicht nur was die Eisenbahn oder den Postverkehr betrifft oder die Migration vom Land in die Stadt, sondern eben auch was die Toten betrifft. Die Toten liegen nicht mehr statisch auf dem Friedhof, sondern sie bewegen sich und beleben sich neu.

Man kann vielleicht ganz pauschal sagen, in den monotheistischen Religionen ist die Feuerbestattung letztlich eine Strafe und nichts Legitimes. Das Judentum begräbt. Das Christentum daraufhin auch. Der Islam begräbt. Die Germanen verbrennen zum Teil. In Indien ist die

Feuerbestattung bis heute ein rezenter Brauch. Die alten Römer haben mitunter verbrannt, es sind aber auch Erdbestattungen nachgewiesen. Dadurch, dass das Römische Reich ein religiös und sozial vielfältiger Raum war, findet man da alle Bestattungsformen. Interessanterweise ist es aber eben tatsächlich so, dass die modernen Feuerbestatter, die des 19. Jahrhunderts, sich auf Rom, auf die Griechen und auf die Germanen und auch auf die Inder berufen und die Feuerbestattung letztlich als den ursprünglicheren Brauch imaginieren, der vom Christentum lediglich verdrängt worden sei. Letztlich ist die Feuerbestattung durch Karl den Großen, also schon im frühen Mittelalter, verboten worden und wenn man in die Geschichte schaut, wurden Ketzer, wurden ketzerische Bücher, wurden Häretiker verbrannt. Hier geht es also auch um eine Form von Reinigung im spirituellen Sinn. Die, von denen geglaubt wurde, sie bedrohten den christlichen Glauben, wurden ins Feuer geschickt. Und das überträgt sich im 19. Jahrhundert ins Materielle. Während im frühneuzeitlichen Europa Hexenverbrennungen stattfanden, hat die Neuzeit diese mikrobielle Reinheit im Blick, nicht mehr die spirituelle Reinheit. Das ist ganz interessant. Das ist also die Verlagerung von der Vormoderne in die Moderne. Da hängt natürlich der ganze naturwissenschaftliche Diskurs dran, die Mikroskope werden entdeckt, mit den Mikroskopen entdeckt man eine Mikrowelt. Man fragt sich, woher eigentlich die Krankheiten kommen. Lange herrschte die Miasmentheorie vor, eine Vorstellung von schlechten Dünsten, die Krankheiten hervorriefen. Irgendwann entdeckt man, es gibt kleine materielle Körperchen, Korpuskel, dann wird das Bakterium entdeckt. So entsteht der neuzeitliche Hygienediskurs um mikrobielle Reinheit, Stärkung der Abwehrkräfte, den gesunden Körper im gesunden Staat. Das ist alles politisiert und kulturell gefärbt.

Die Erde gilt den Feuerbestattern als das langsame Element, das mit dem Weiblichen verbunden ist, aber nicht nur mit dem Weiblichen, sondern eben auch mit dem Klerus, also mit allem, was in diesem säkularistischen Diskurs als vormodern abgeurteilt wird. Die Erde wird als das Langsame, Verwesende, Dünstende, Undurchsichtige, Drückende, auch Enge gedeutet. Das findet auch Übertragung auf den Mutterschoß. Auch er symbolisiert diese dunkle Enge, aus der sich der neue Mensch in Richtung Licht befreien muss. Im Feuerbestattungsdiskurs steht dem das schnelle, beschleunigende, männlich kodierte Element gegenüber. Männliche und weibliche Kodierungen stehen sich also im Feuerbestattungsdiskurs des 19. Jahrhunderts gegenüber und sind auch mit den Elementen verbunden. Im religiösen Kontext dominiert die Vorstellung, dass die Toten in den Boden, ja in die Erde der Väter entlassen werden. In der Feuerbestattung dreht sich das um. Das wird in meinem Buch auch eine Rolle spielen. Dass sozusagen dieser Genderdiskurs des 19. Jahrhunderts sich in der Feuerbestattung auf den Tod ausweitet.

Da geht es viel um Bewegung und Raumbezüge. Wenn der tote Körper in die Erde gelassen wird und dort auch verfällt, dann ist der Körper noch eine ganze Weile materiell präsent. Eigentlich ähnlich wie bei Shiva und Sheloshim, von denen wir vorhin sprachen. Und so ist es auch beim Verfall des toten Körpers. Er ist erst noch ganz materiell da und verfällt immer weiter. Anders wenn man eine Urne in die Erde oder eben nicht in die Erde gibt, sondern sie im Columbarium aufstellt, dann ist das Endprodukt schon da. Es gibt keine Veränderung mehr. Insofern – und das ist durchaus auch ein zeitgenössischer Diskurs – ist sozusagen die langsame Verwesung in der Erde ein dem Menschen näherer Prozess, ein naturnaher Prozess, der auch mit unseren Emotionen, mit unseren

Trauergefühlen korrespondiert. Wir sind am Anfang eben besonders betroffen und je mehr Zeit vergeht, umso stärker sind wir vielleicht auch wieder vom Alltag absorbiert. Das ist sozusagen eine Rhythmik, die vielleicht mit der Vormoderne konnotiert ist. Und jetzt müsste man mit Günter Anders kommen und fragen, ist der Mensch eigentlich antiquiert? Also überholen wir uns sozusagen mit unserer Technik, mit unserer Technisierung letztlich selbst und entspricht das gar nicht mehr unserer eigenen Rhythmik? Mit solchen Fragen sah sich schon das 19. Jahrhundert konfrontiert. Nämlich die, mit welchen Emotionen man ans Erdgrab tritt und mit welchen ans Urnengrab. Und das sind unterschiedliche Emotionen. Bei der Urne, so machen es die Quellenschriften der Zeit deutlich, eher distanziert, würdigend, aber nicht mehr in dieser emotionalen Betroffenheit, während die Emotionen am Erdgrab präsenter sind. Dabei wollen die Zeitgenossen starke Emotionen ja gerne hinter sich lassen, sie verstanden sich ja als progressiv, aufgeklärt, nicht als überbordend oder nicht zu kontrollierend emotional, wie sie sich etwa Klageweiber vorstellen.

Das erste deutsche Krematorium, das zur Anwendung kam, hat Friedrich Siemens gebaut. Und das ist auch vielfach beworben worden, das finden wir zum Beispiel in der bürgerlichen Familienzeitschrift *Gartenlaube*. Hier existiert eine Abbildung, auf der ein protestantischer Pfarrer den Sarg einsegnet. Der wird aber nicht mehr in die Erde herabgelassen, sondern praktisch in die Verbrennungskammer hinabgelassen, sodass dieser Moment des Hinablassens, des Abschiednehmens letztlich kopiert wird, nur dass es in Richtung Technik geht, nicht mehr in Richtung dieser langsamen Verwesung in der Erde. Ja, und es wurde als unästhetisch oder als nicht statthaft empfunden, dass nach dieser Aussegnung, nach diesem

Abschiednehmen dann unten in diesem Raum, in diesem Verbrennungsraum, Helfer den Sarg vor der Einäscherung nochmals anfassen. Dann hat Siemens also einen Mechanismus ersonnen, der diesen Moment der Unsicherheit überbrückt. Das heißt, das ist letztlich die Technik, die die Unsicherheit, wie mit den Toten nach der Verabschiedung, aber vor der Einäscherung in der Feuerbestattung umzugehen ist, überbrückt. Der Sarg wird herabgelassen und durch ein Rollensystem in den Ofen transportiert, sodass keine menschliche Hand ihn mehr berührt, sondern erst die Asche, die ja ein Produkt, ein menschliches Produkt, ein menschlich geschaffenes Produkt ist, wieder von Menschenhand eingesammelt und in die Urne gegeben werden darf. Und das fand ich sehr eingängig, dass es da offenbar eine Debatte darum gab und dass sich die zeitgenössischen Feuerbestatter befangen fühlten. Dieses Berührungsreglement ist meiner Ansicht nach ganz sinnfällig für den Umgang der säkularen Feuerbestatter mit dem Tod.

MARIA CLARA MARTINELLI: ON BURIAL CULTURES IN PREHISTORY*

The Aeolian Islands are named after Aeolus, who was a mythological king and a patriarch in antiquity. He had his palace, and therefore his kingdom, in the acropolis of Lipari, which sits on a natural cliff, defended by tall, rocky crags jutting out into the sea. In the *Odyssey*, Homer describes it as fortified by gilded bronze walls, an image likely suggested by the reflection of the sun's rays off the red rock that makes up the "Rocca" of Lipari. The Aeolian Islands are thus a site of very ancient myths reaching back into the Bronze Age.

A burial place is natural. At some point, human communities decided or felt the need to bury their loved ones; this has been occurring since the earliest prehistoric times. The oldest burial sites date back as far as the Paleolithic Era. In Lipari, the need to bury the dead has returned to us in more recent times as some of the most important archaeological evidence we have from the Aeolian Islands: a necropolis used during the Greek and Roman periods from the sixth century BCE to the sixth century CE, which is abundant in burial sites of various types.

The islands were first inhabited during the Neolithic Era, after the middle of the sixth millennium BCE, that is, between 5,500 and 5,000 years before Christ. While the oldest burial sites on these islands date back to the Neolithic period, only a few of them were found. During this period, tombs were composed of a pit bordered by stone slabs, into which the body was placed in a crouched position.

*This text is based on the transcript of a research interview.

Other finds from prehistoric times include evidence of the use of incineration. Toward the end of the Bronze Age, this practice was used in the same necropolis in close proximity to other burial rituals, including cremation and inhumation *entro pithos*, or burial by placing the corpse in a crouching position into a large vessel. The large vessel clearly represents an important symbol, that of the maternal womb, the source of life. Hence death recalls birth and, therefore, a return to life.

Greek and Roman necropolises were quite extensive, and abounded in tombs of various kinds, especially sarcophagi in clay or stone. The funeral ritual involved placing grave goods outside or sometimes even inside the tomb to accompany the deceased on their journey to the afterlife. In the Greek necropolis, the rituals of both incineration and inhumation, were used. The inhumed were placed in sarcophagi; the cremated were placed as ashes in jars. It depended on the respective beliefs and rituals, as the two burial methods were not always contemporaneously in use.

The human community buries the individual who has died. Since prehistoric times, when an important person in the community was buried, the accompanying funeral ritual would involve placing a set of personal objects and ornaments in the grave. Over time, social differences consolidated and extended to entire dominant groups. Even in the Greek and Roman periods, as the custom of burying one's dead spread throughout society, social differentiation based on wealth and family rank remained. Cremation is a ritual that developed over time, while the inhumation of the body after death was the first form of funerary ritual.

Consider the Chinchorro mummies, from a ritual used in northern Chile. There, the dead were not buried, but left exposed to the air so that the bodies would mummify. The extremely hot and dry climate made this process possible, and thus it became their custom. In every human community there is a very strong relationship between the group members and the place where they live since the natural environment greatly conditions human life.

Death is one of life's many mysteries. No one wants to accept that they must die, so acknowledging that your life is finite is a major step. It is much easier and more comforting to imagine that, after death, your life can be better than the one you have now. And then there is memory: the desire among those who are alive to remember, to commemorate, to remain close to those who have died. That is why loved ones and those important to the community are buried. To bury those you have been close to is a form of comfort for those who remain living. It enables them to be near their loved ones even after they have died.

To be able to accept death, it must be rendered very symbolic. In other words, you have to create a lot of scenography to strengthen, conversely, life itself. Think about the imperial tomb of Emperor Qin in Xi'an, China: with his terracotta army, he created something magnificent, unparalleled in any other culture, purely to satisfy his impossible desire for immortality.

When you excavate graves, you can sense the great respect it involves. First of all, there is a respect for what you are uncovering. Then comes the interest in the discovery itself, in the grave goods and what this particular tomb may preserve. Even with the most ancient tombs from prehistoric times, extreme attention is given during excavation to keeping whatever remains as fully intact as possible. We need to gather as much information from them as we can, since for those who study ancient history both the excavation site and the found objects represent non-written sources that are highly significant for the understanding of our past. In the graves, not only the objects but also the skeletons are important for research, which can now use DNA analysis to derive information on populations, health, and diseases. It is also possible to analyze vessel interiors and identify the funeral goods placed in the tomb, detecting traces of food or other substances such as aromatic oils, as such vessels contained offerings for the deceased to accompany them on their journey into the afterlife.

Archaeology studies a past that no longer exists. Not only do the people no longer exist, but even the cultures represented by those people no longer exist. However, it is our own history and a relatively brief one at that; it hasn't been very long since the Homo sapiens emerged. Yet, it is possible to study the past—in the present epoch, we have so many more communication tools than our predecessors did. For archaeologists, objects of everyday use, which we refer to as comprising "material culture," enable us to retell the past. With the introduction of writing, everything became faster and more manipulable. Today, this velocity makes us forget rapidly. It is my observation that the speed of communication is directly related to the speed of forgetting. Archaeology serves the process of remembering by reconstructing our most ancient history.

Human cultures convey traces, and it is the archaeologist's task to look for these messages of the past. The interest in rediscovery, in archaeology, is actually quite recent. There was no such interest in the past—settlements were often reused or quarried for materials to construct other buildings. I'm thinking of, for example, the walls of Greek cities, as in the case of Lipari, which were dismantled during the Middle Ages to gain building materials for the monastery. Another such instance, also in Lipari, is the large Greek and Roman cemetery—its deepest strata rests on prehistoric settlements, which were destroyed in this way.

Here in Lipari we talk about mythical kingdoms, but you also have to consider the politics of power: the longer your lineage, the more respect you get. That is why ancestry is so important to elite groups in society.

Well, it is better not to think about it, even though I think that in our own time old age sparks more fear than death itself. Death, in any case, is irreversible—we realize this, don't we? While old age occurs during life and leads to death—that's the message of science, anyway—religion guides us to think of death as a solution, a beautiful moment leading to another life, in a world different from the one we experience as real. Still, death is not something one gets used to quite so easily.

MARIA CLARA MARTINELLI: LE CULTURE FUNERARIE NELLA PREISTORIA*

Le isole Eolie prendono il nome da Eolo, che era un re e un patriarca della mitologia antica. Eolo aveva la sua reggia, e quindi il suo regno, sull'acropoli di Lipari. L'acropoli di Lipari è una rupe naturale difesa da alte balze rocciose protese sul mare. Nell'*Odissea* di Omero si può leggere di "mura di bronzo", un'immagine questa probabilmente data dal riflesso del sole sulla roccia rossa che compone la rocca di Lipari. Le Eolie dunque sono un luogo di miti molto antichi, le cui basi affondano addirittura nell'età del bronzo.

Un luogo sepolcrale è qualcosa di naturale. A un certo punto le comunità umane sentirono il bisogno di seppellire i propri cari. È così fin dalla preistoria più remota. I sepolcri più antichi risalgono al paleolitico. In epoche più recenti, a Lipari, la necessità di seppellire ha restituito una delle testimonianze archeologiche più importanti delle isole Eolie: una necropoli che è stata usata sia in età greca che in età romana, dal VI secolo avanti Cristo fino al VI secolo dopo Cristo, e che dunque è ricchissima di sepolture di vari tipi.

Le isole Eolie sono state abitate per la prima volta nel neolitico. Le sepolture più antiche che si trovano sulle isole risalgono a dopo la metà del VI millennio, fra il 5500 e il 5000 avanti Cristo. Alcune sono ancora più antiche, ma sono pochissime. In questo periodo, la tomba era una fossa delimitata da lastre di pietra, in cui la persona veniva deposta rannicchiata. Nella preistoria, si trovano anche

*Questo testo si basa sulla trascrizione di un'intervista di ricerca.

altre testimonianze, tra cui l'uso dell'incinerazione, che alla fine dell'età del bronzo è attestata in una necropoli a "rito misto". Questo vuol dire che nello stesso periodo erano presenti sia i riti dell'incinerazione che dell'inumazione *entro pithos*, e cioè dentro un grande vaso nel quale l'inumato veniva deposto rannicchiato. Chiaramente il grande vaso rappresenta un importante simbolo, quello della maternità, fonte di vita. La morte, pertanto, posizionata dentro questo vaso, è un richiamo alla nascita e quindi un ritorno alla vita.

A Lipari, la necropoli greca e romana è molto estesa e molto ricca di tombe di vario genere, soprattutto a sarcofago, in argilla oppure in pietra. Il rito funerario consisteva nel deporre un corredo all'esterno o anche all'interno della tomba, che doveva accompagnare il defunto nel suo viaggio verso l'aldilà. Anche nella necropoli greca venivano usati due riti, sia l'incinerazione che l'inumazione: l'inumazione nel sarcofago, le ceneri in vasi. Si tratta di una questione di credenze e di riti, infatti i due modi di seppellire non sempre sono stati impiegati contemporaneamente.

La comunità seppellisce il singolo individuo. Fin dalla preistoria, quando si seppelliva una persona importante, un corredo di oggetti e ornamenti personali veniva riposto nella fossa. Nel tempo, le differenze sociali si consolidarono e simili costumi furono estesi ad interi gruppi dominanti. Quando in epoca greca e romana i riti funerari si diffusero ampiamente nella società, differenze di rango e di ricchezza nel trattamento dei morti rimasero tali. Fu la sepoltura a costituire la prima forma rituale funeraria, mentre l'incinerazione è un rito che si sviluppò nel tempo.

Presso i Chinchorro, nel Cile del nord, i defunti non vengono seppelliti, vengono esposti all'aria finché diventano mummie. È un processo possibile grazie al clima estremamente caldo e secco. Lì si usa fare così. Ogni comunità instaura un rapporto molto forte con il luogo in cui vive perché la natura condiziona moltissimo la vita dell'uomo.

La morte è uno dei tanti misteri della vita dell'uomo. Non si vuole mai accettare di morire. Accettare che la tua vita sia finita è una grande consapevolezza. È più facile e confortante pensare che dopo la morte si possa avere una vita migliore di quella che si è avuta in realtà. E poi c'è il ricordo, il voler commemorare, il voler stare vicini ai morti, il desiderio di seppellire le persone più care e quelle più importanti per la comunità. Insomma, seppellire coloro ai quali si è stati vicini è una forma di conforto per chi rimane in vita.

La morte, per poterla accettare, la devi rendere molto simbolica, le devi creare una scenografia per rafforzare, al contrario, proprio la vita. Si pensi per esempio alla tomba dell'imperatore Qin, a Xi'an, in Cina: facendosi seppellire con un esercito di terracotta ha fatto una cosa che per ricchezza non ha eguali nelle culture del mondo solo per soddisfare il desiderio impossibile di essere immortale.

C'è un grande rispetto quando si scavano le tombe. Prima di tutto c'è il rispetto per quello che stai scoprendo. Poi c'è la novità, l'interesse per la scoperta in sé, per il corredo, per quello che conserva la tomba. Anche per le tombe più antiche, quelle della preistoria, c'è un'estrema attenzione nello scavo così da conservare nel modo più integro ciò che rimane. Per chi studia la storia antica, lo scavo stesso così come gli oggetti ritrovati rappresentano fonti non scritte molto importanti per conoscere il nostro passato. Bisogna trarne il più informazioni possibili.

Poi c'è lo studio degli scheletri. Nelle sepolture, lo studio del DNA è molto importante perché ci fornisce informazioni sulle popolazioni, sulla loro salute e sulle loro malattie. In fine, è possibile anche analizzare il contenuto del corredo, nei cui vasi spesso si trovano tracce di cibo, oli profumati, o altre sostanze che venivano offerte al defunto per affrontare il suo viaggio verso l'aldilà.

L'archeologia studia un passato che non esiste più; non solo le persone non esistono più, ma anche le culture da esse rappresentate. La nostra storia è una storia ancora breve, perché in fondo non è da molto che si è affermato l'*homo sapiens*. In questa nostra epoca abbiamo molti più strumenti per comunicare. Nel passato erano molti meno. Per un archeologo, sono gli oggetti usati quotidianamente che permettono di raccontare il passato, quelli che definiamo "cultura materiale". Con la scrittura, tutto diventò più veloce e più facile da manipolare. Oggi questa velocità ci fa dimenticare in fretta. La velocità nella comunicazione è legata alla velocità nel dimenticare. L'archeologia serve a ricordare ricostruendo la storia più antica.

Le culture umane trasmettono dei messaggi ed è compito dell'archeologo quello di cercare queste tracce del passato. L'interesse verso le scoperte archeologiche è una cosa relativamente recente. Nel passato non esisteva questo interesse, anzi, molto spesso gli insediamenti del passato venivano usati come cave di pietra per costruire nuovi edifici. Si pensi, per esempio, alle cinte murarie della città greca che, nel caso di Lipari, in età medievale furono smantellate per trarne materiale da costruzione con il quale erigere il monastero; oppure, sempre a Lipari, al grande cimitero greco e romano, che negli strati più profondi si trova su di insediamenti preistorici che furono distrutti.

Quando si parla di regni mitici, come nel caso di Lipari, c'è anche una politica del potere che bisogna considerare, e cioè, che più si ha potere, più si ottiene rispetto. Da qui deriva l'importanza dei lignaggi tra i gruppi elitari della società.

Ai nostri tempi, io credo che la vecchiaia faccia molta più paura della morte; la vecchiaia avviene nel corso della vita e conduce verso la morte. La morte è irreversibile – o per lo meno questo è il messaggio della scienza. La religione invece ci porta a pensare alla morte come ad una soluzione, ad un momento bello che ci porterà a vivere in un'altra vita, una vita diversa però, una vita in un mondo che non è quello reale. La morte rimane comunque una cosa a cui è difficile abituarsi.

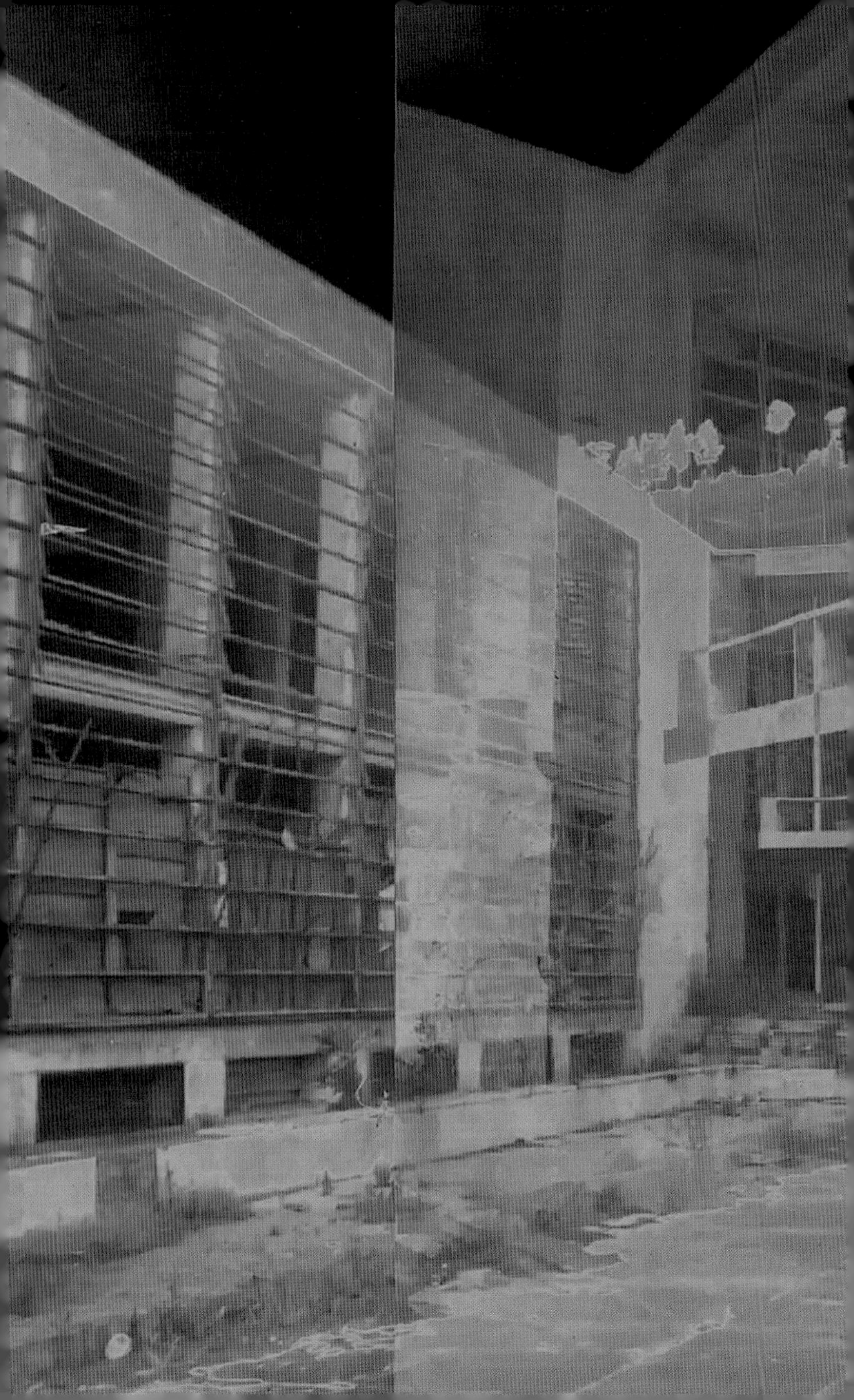

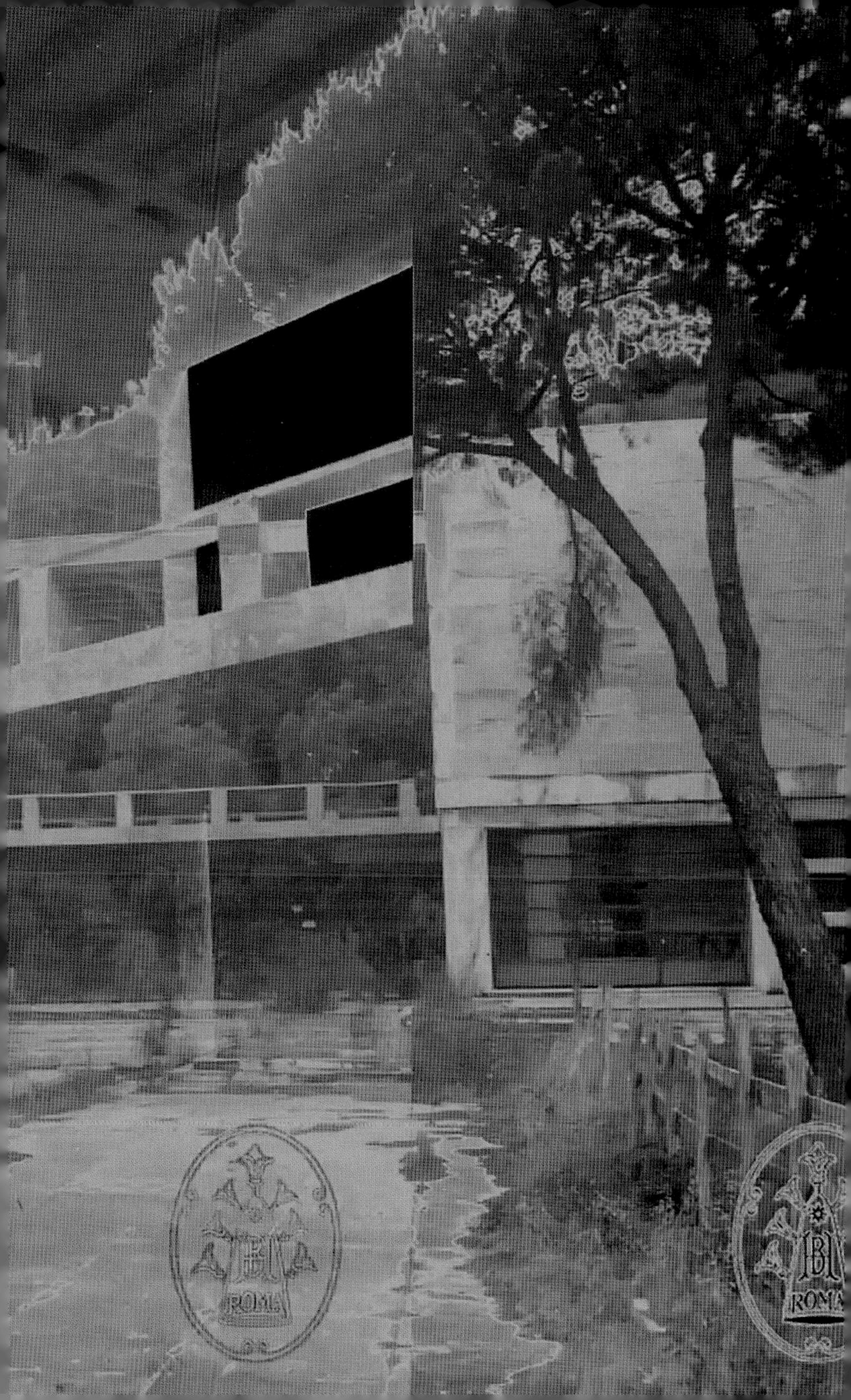

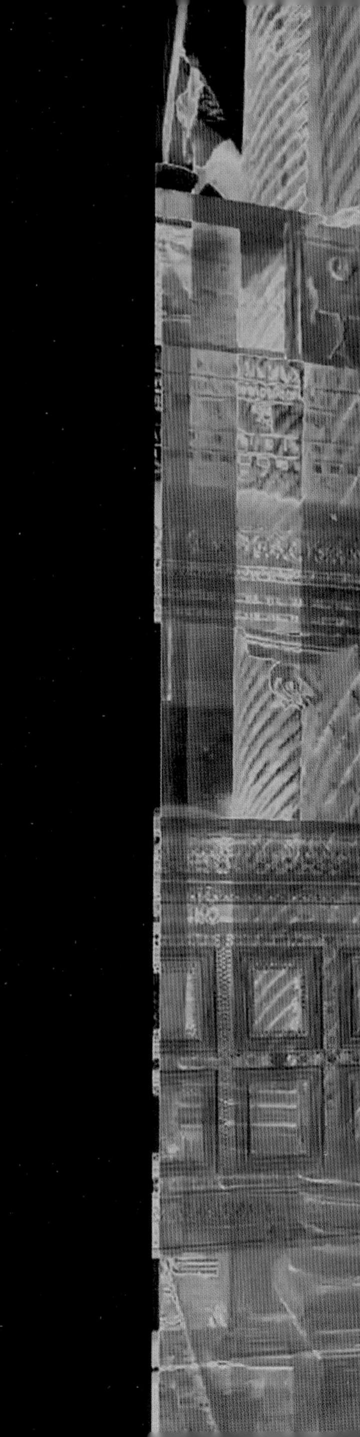

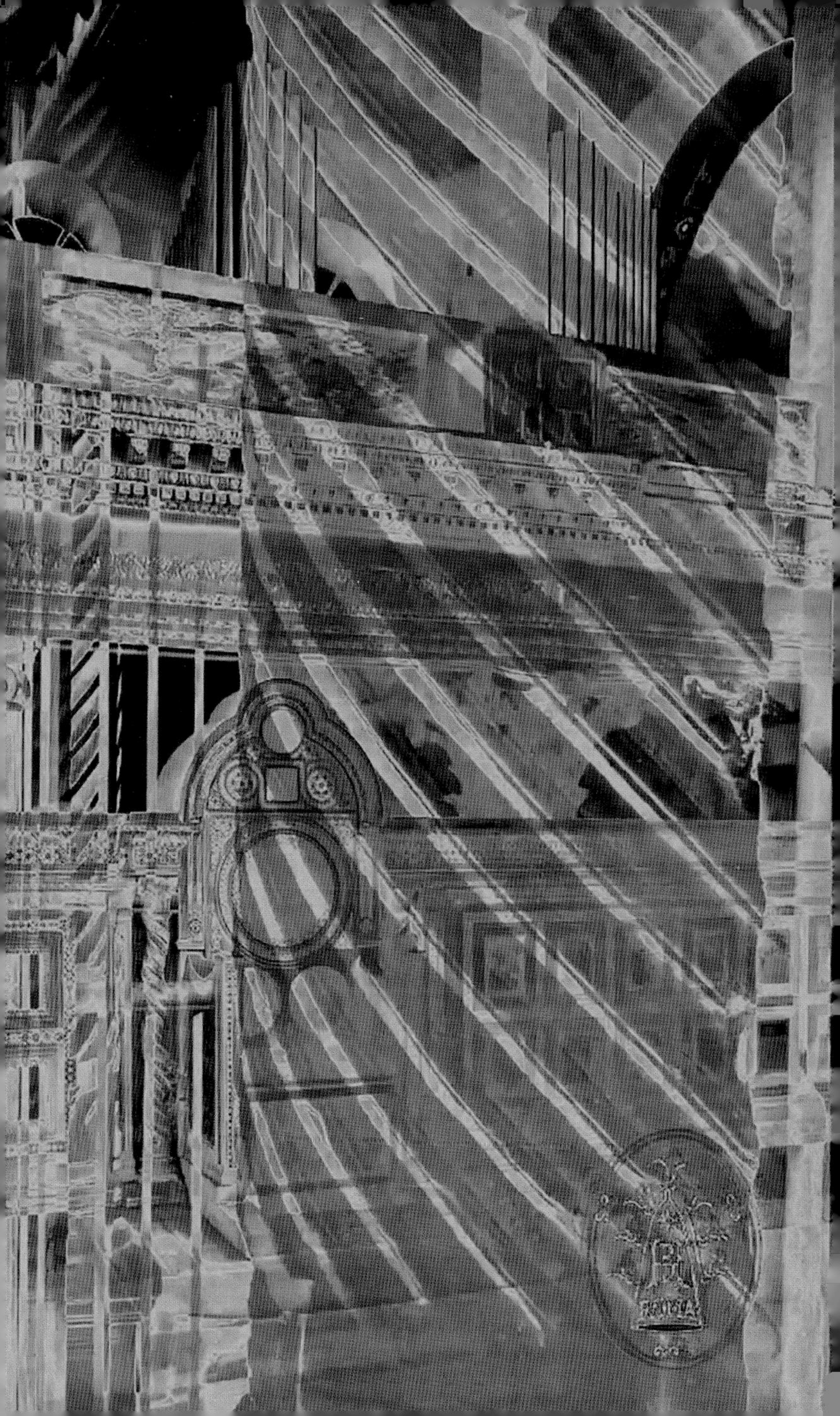

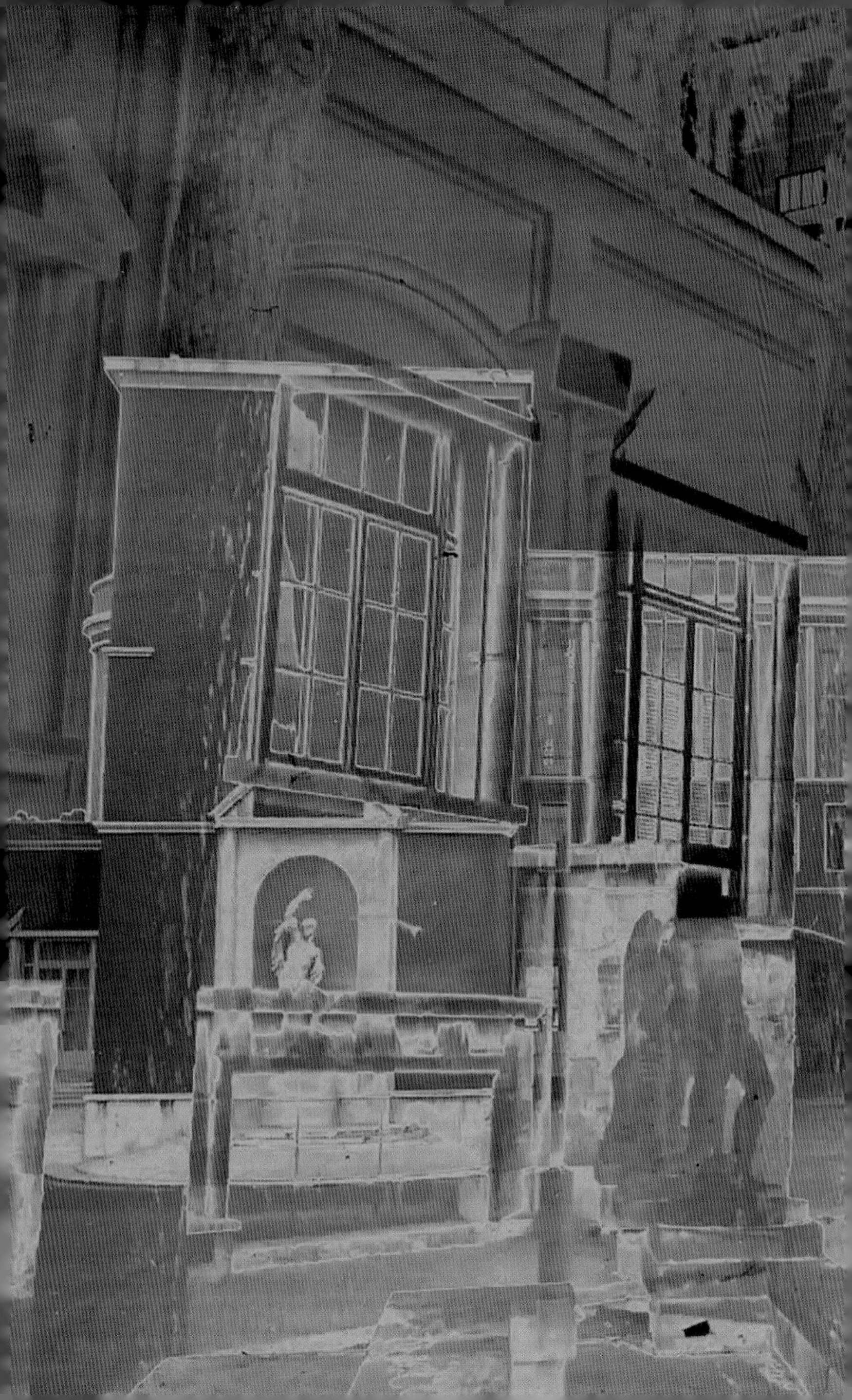

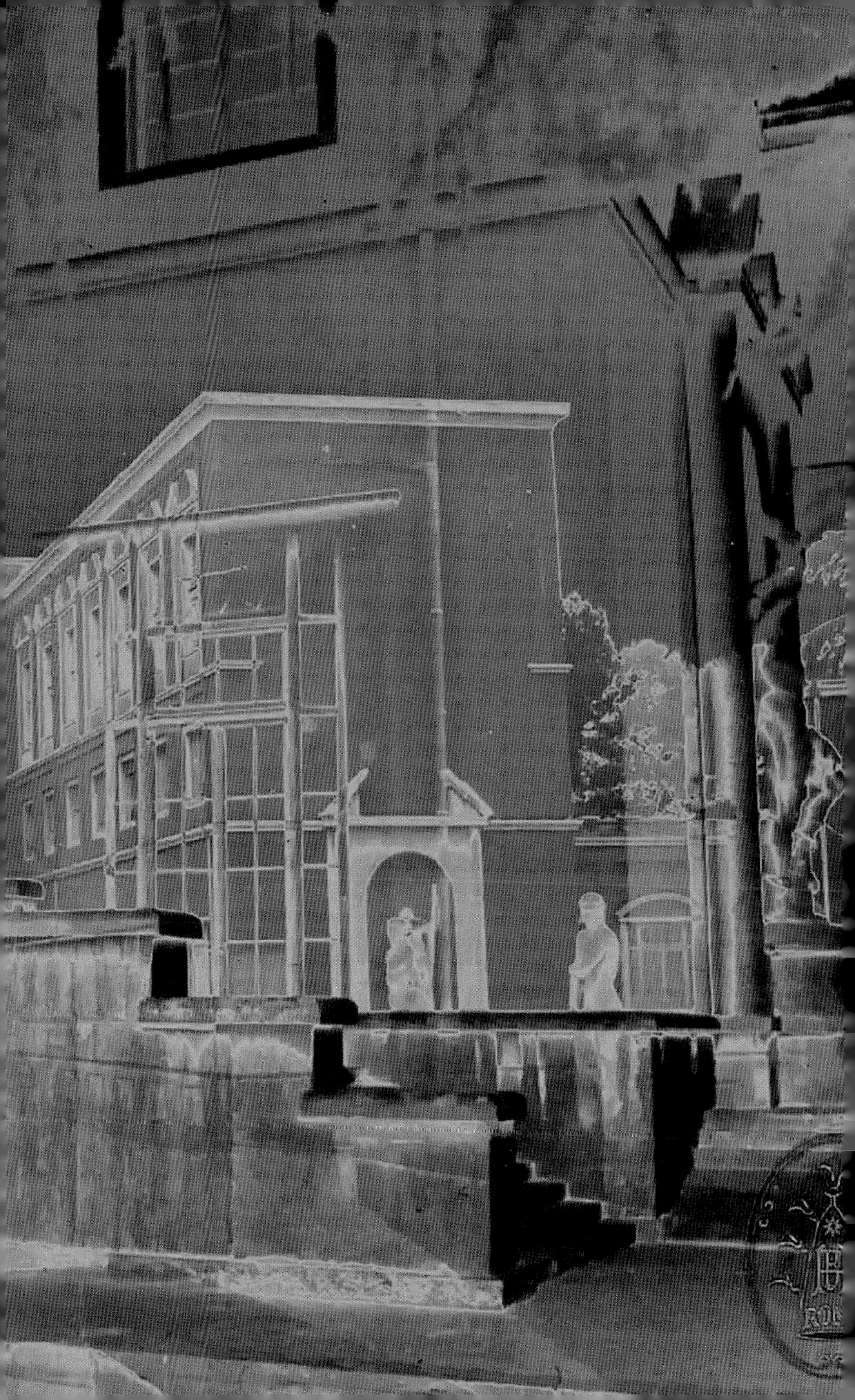

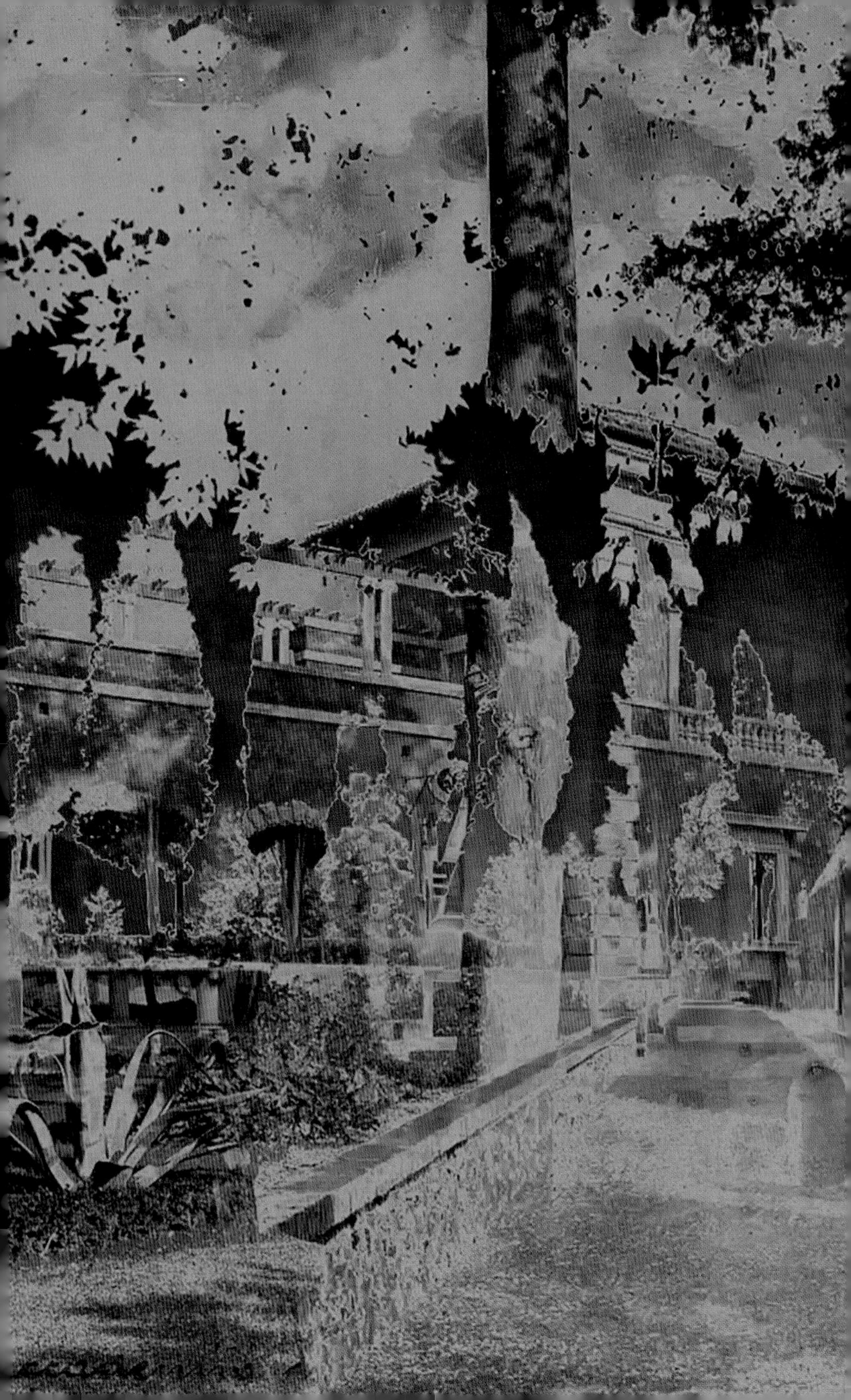

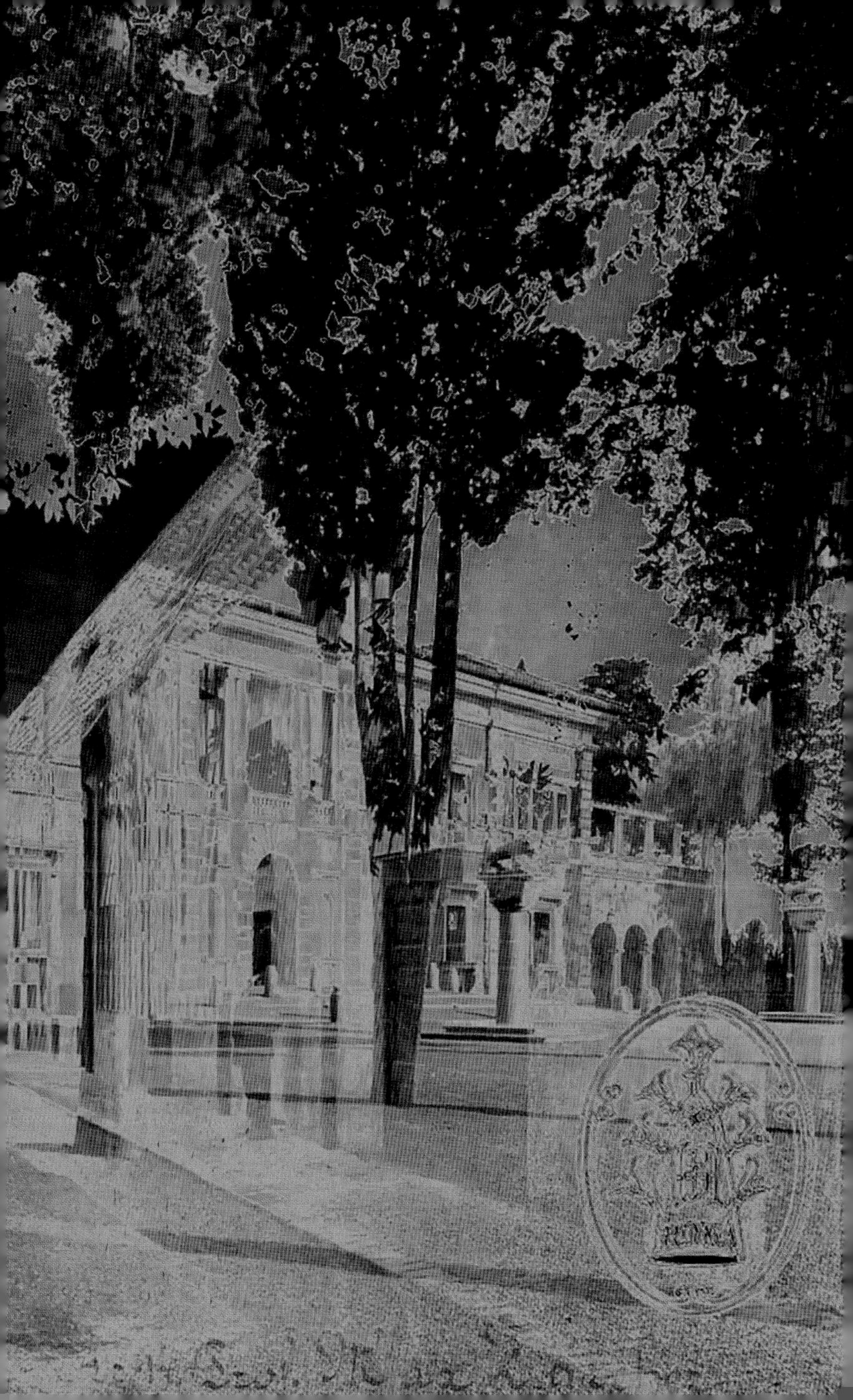

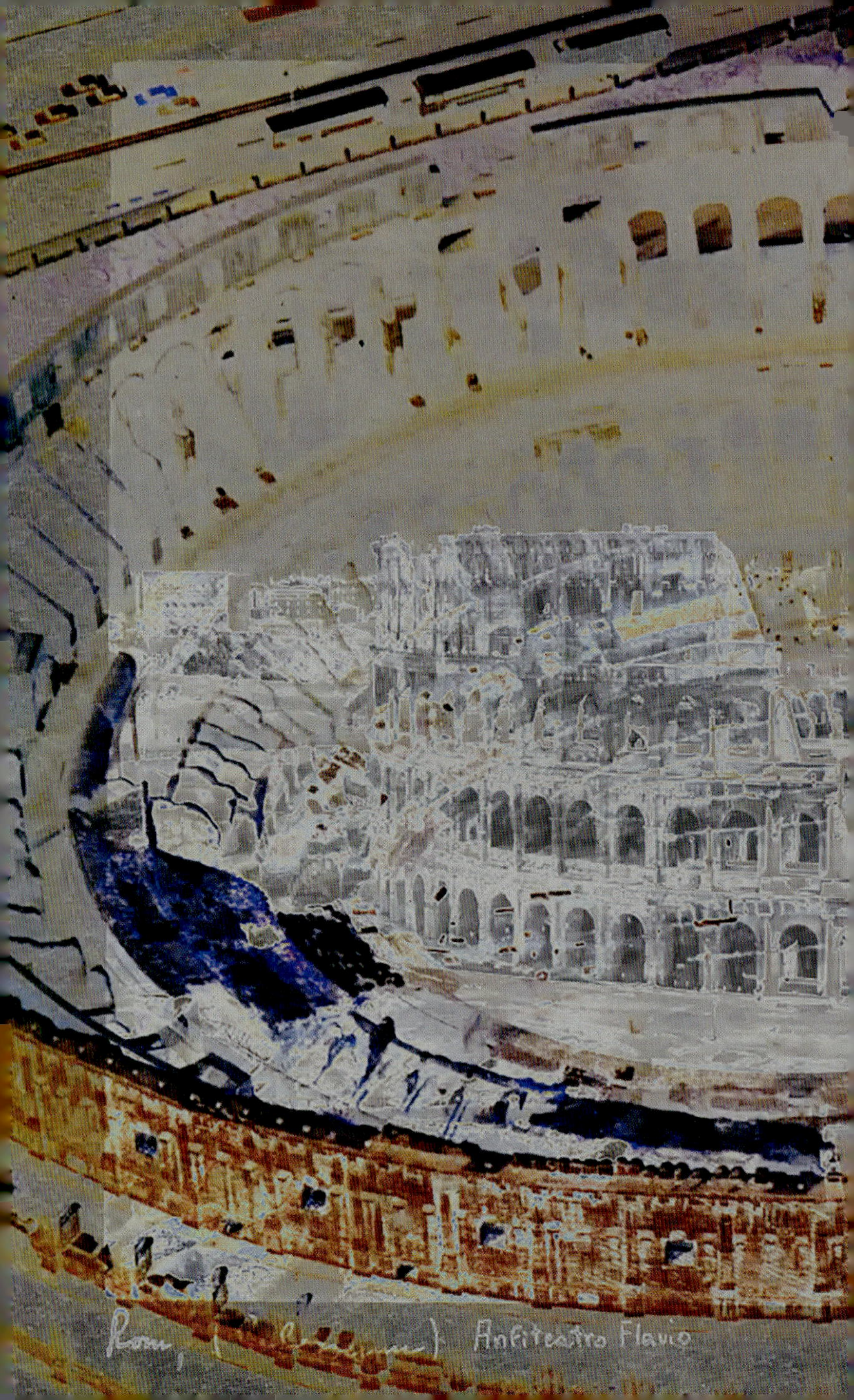
Anfiteatro Flavio

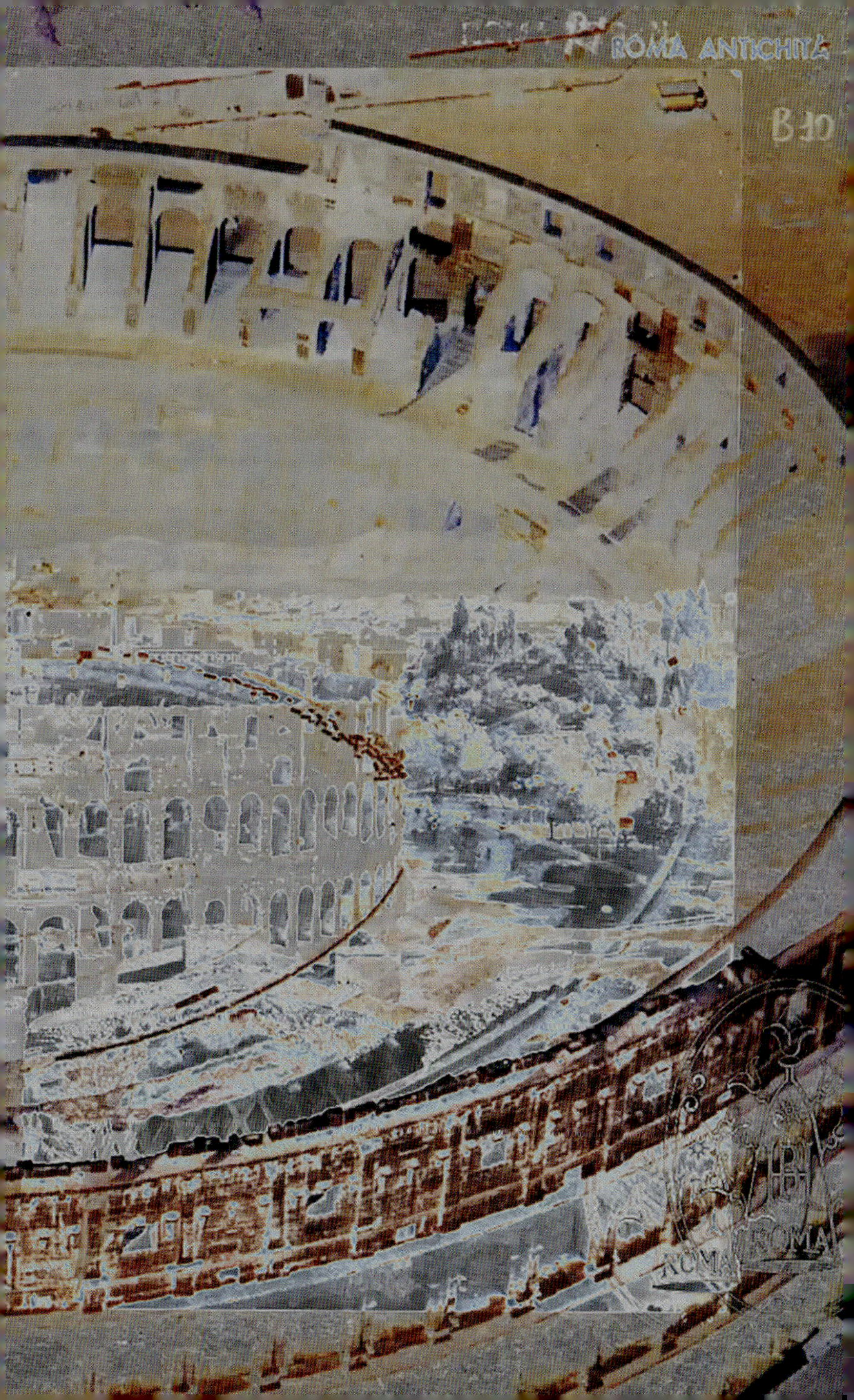
ROMA ANTICHITÀ
B 10

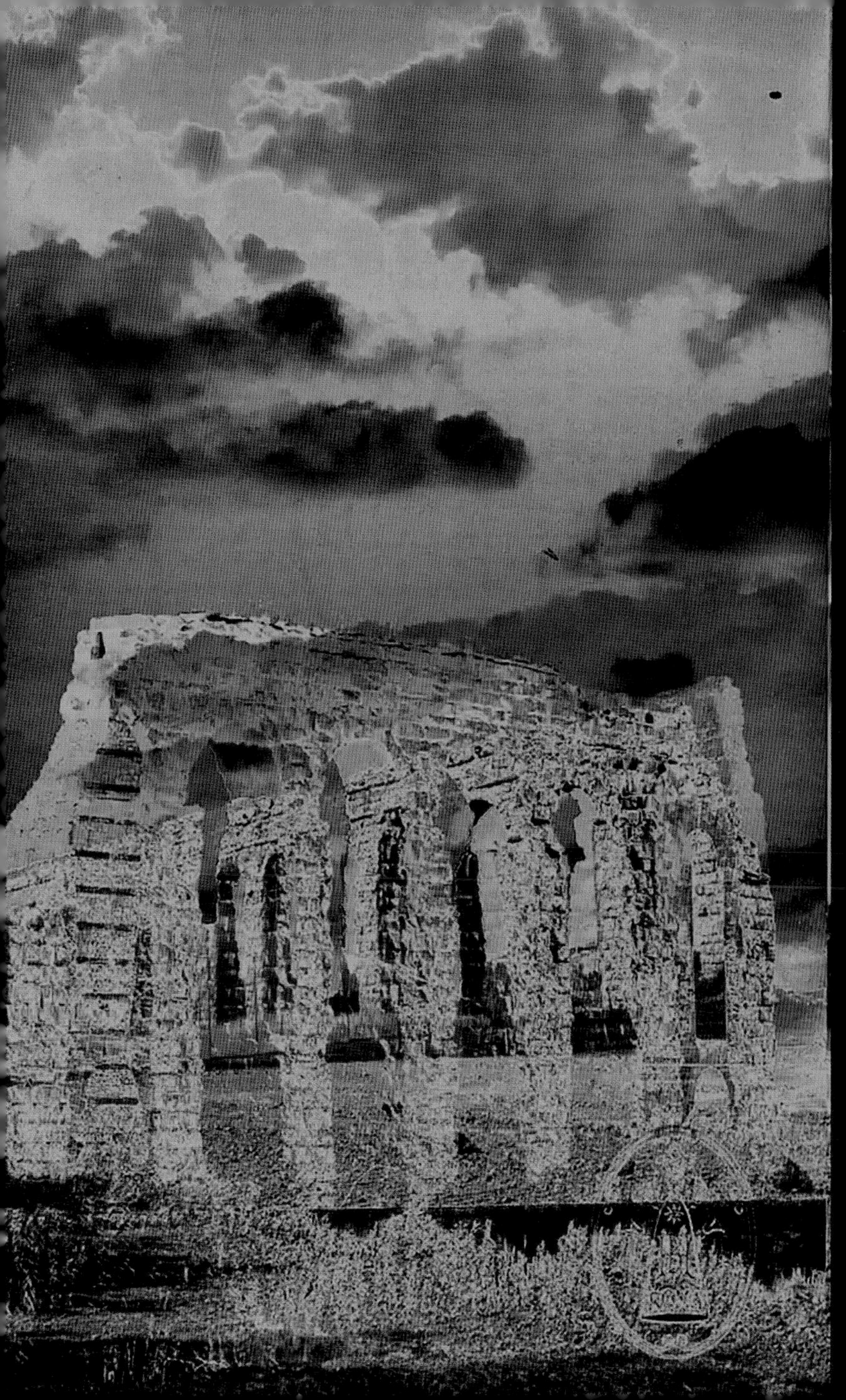

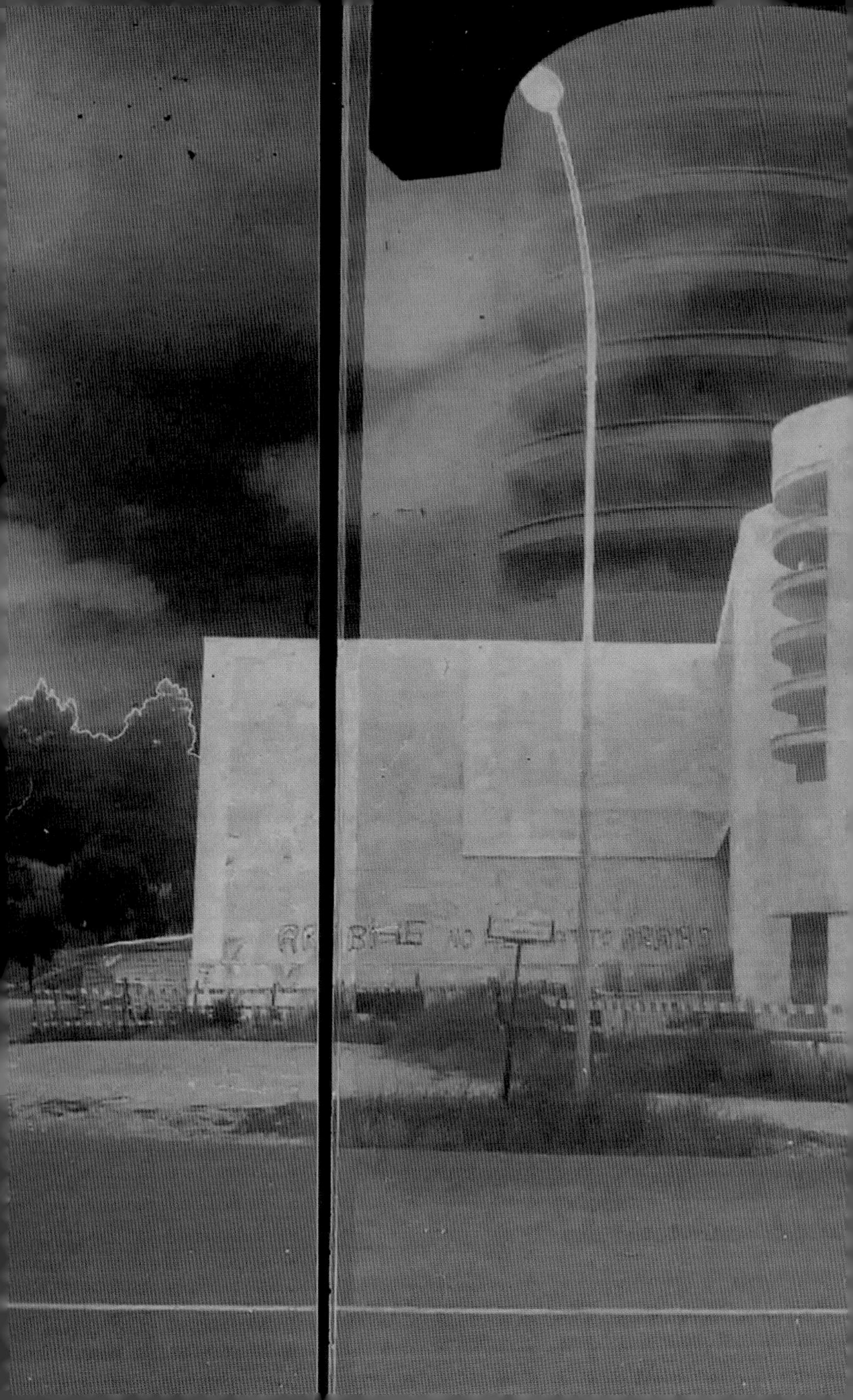

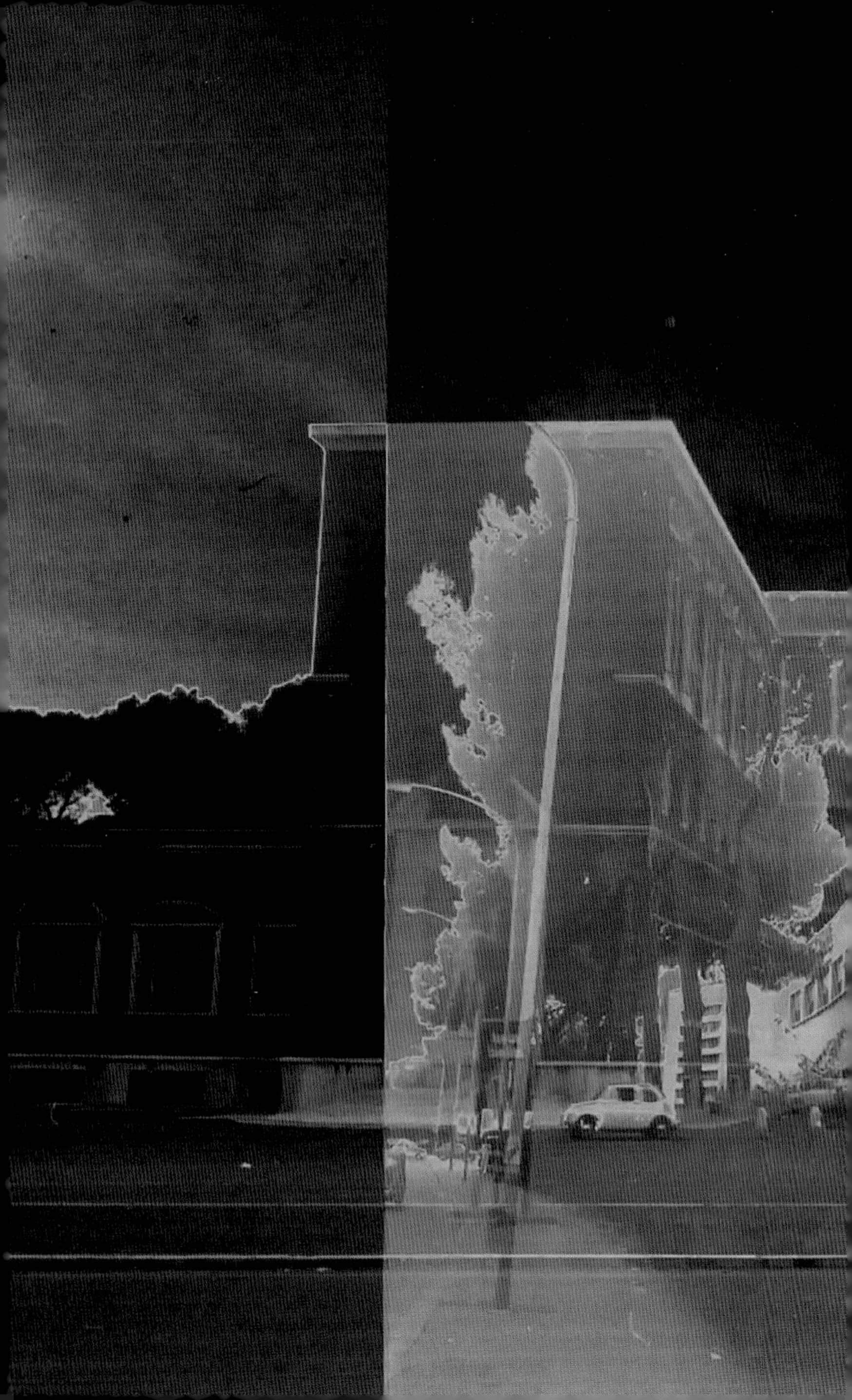

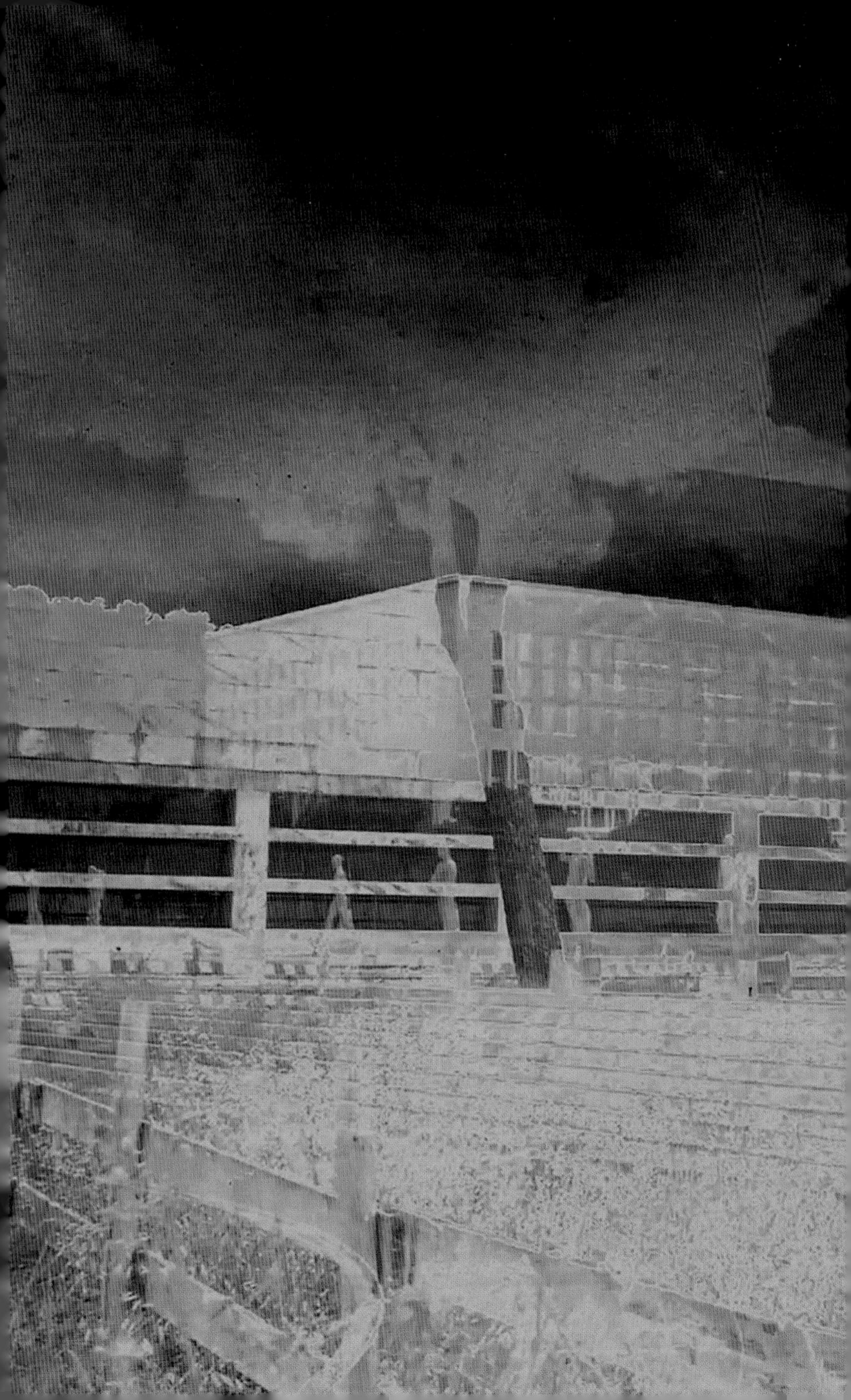

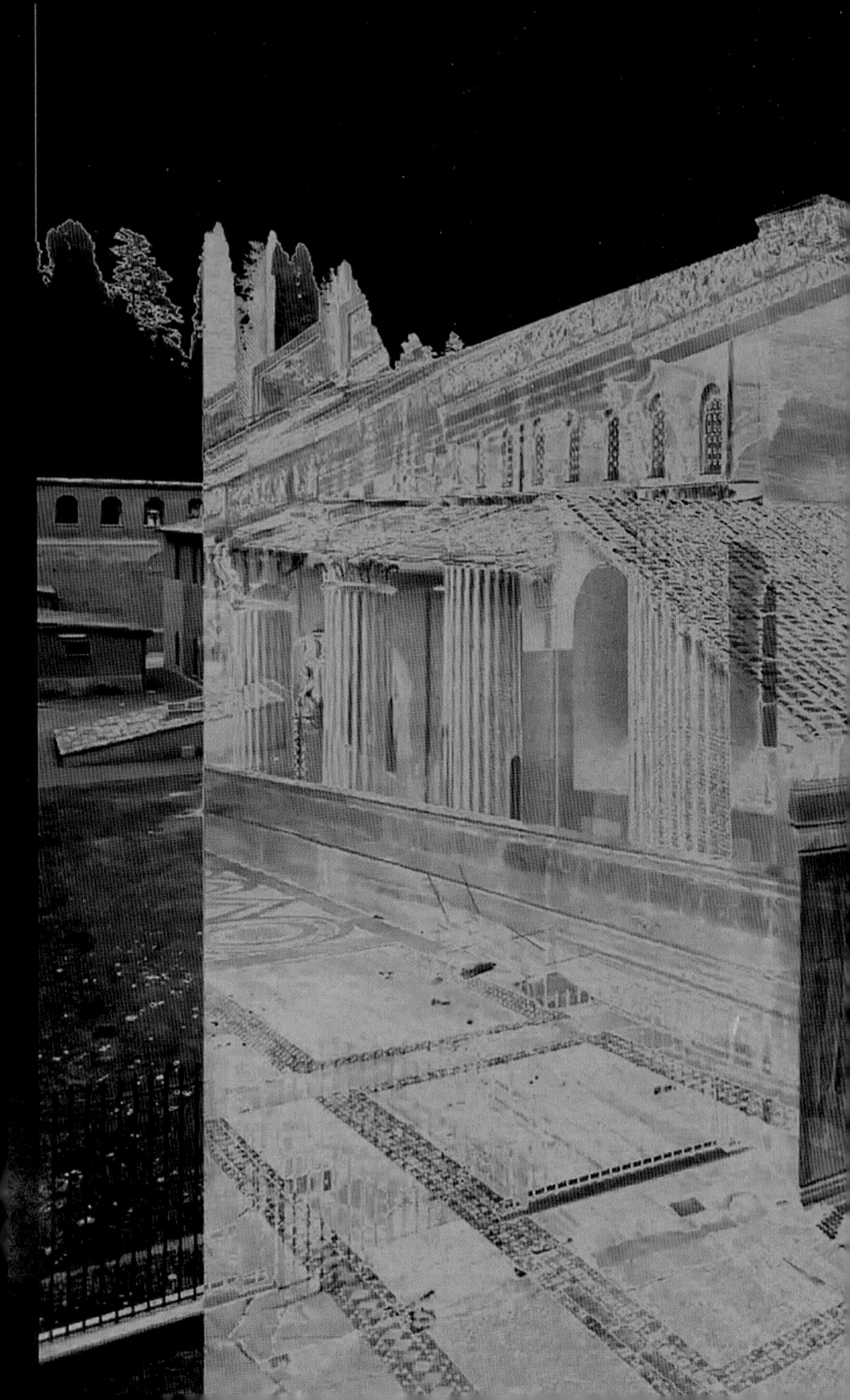

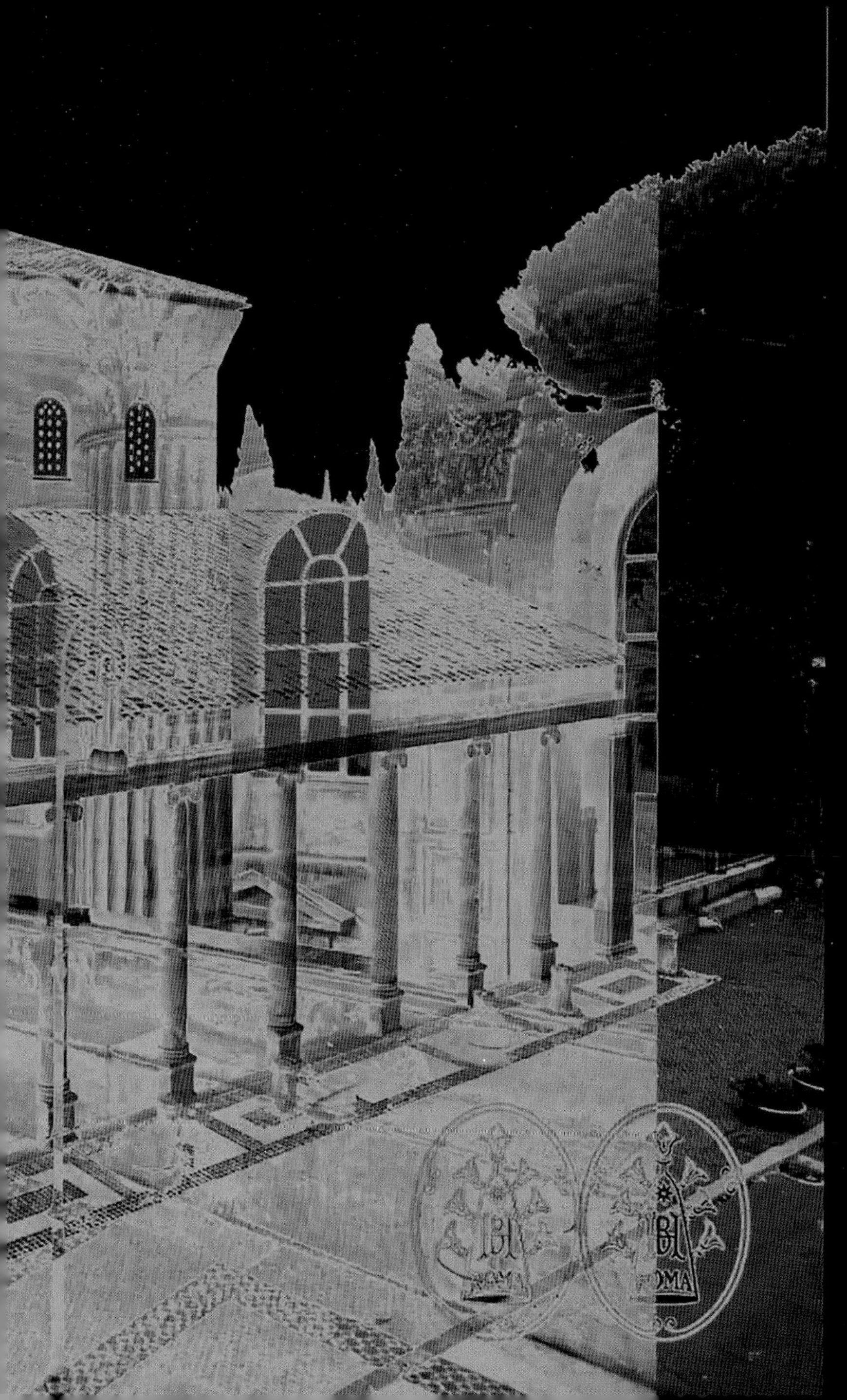

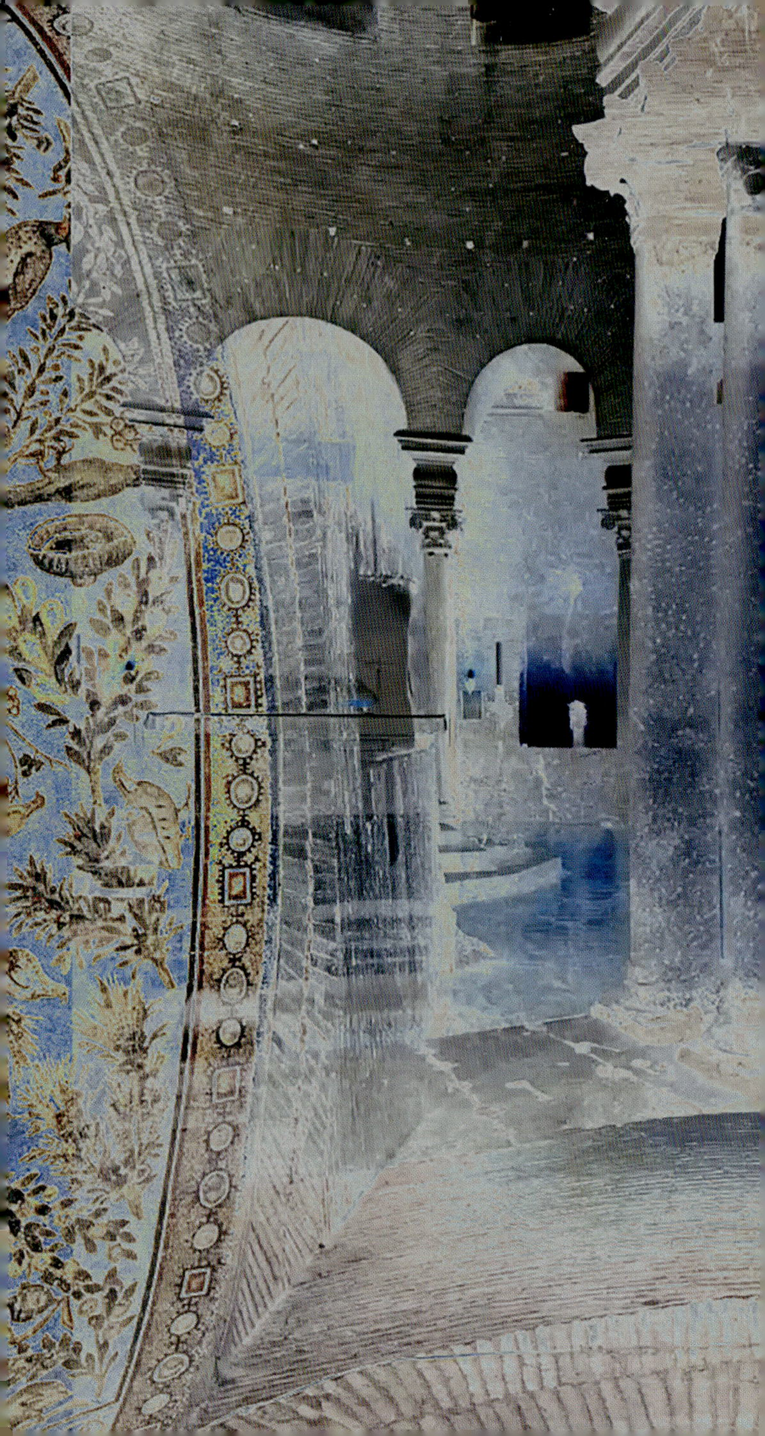

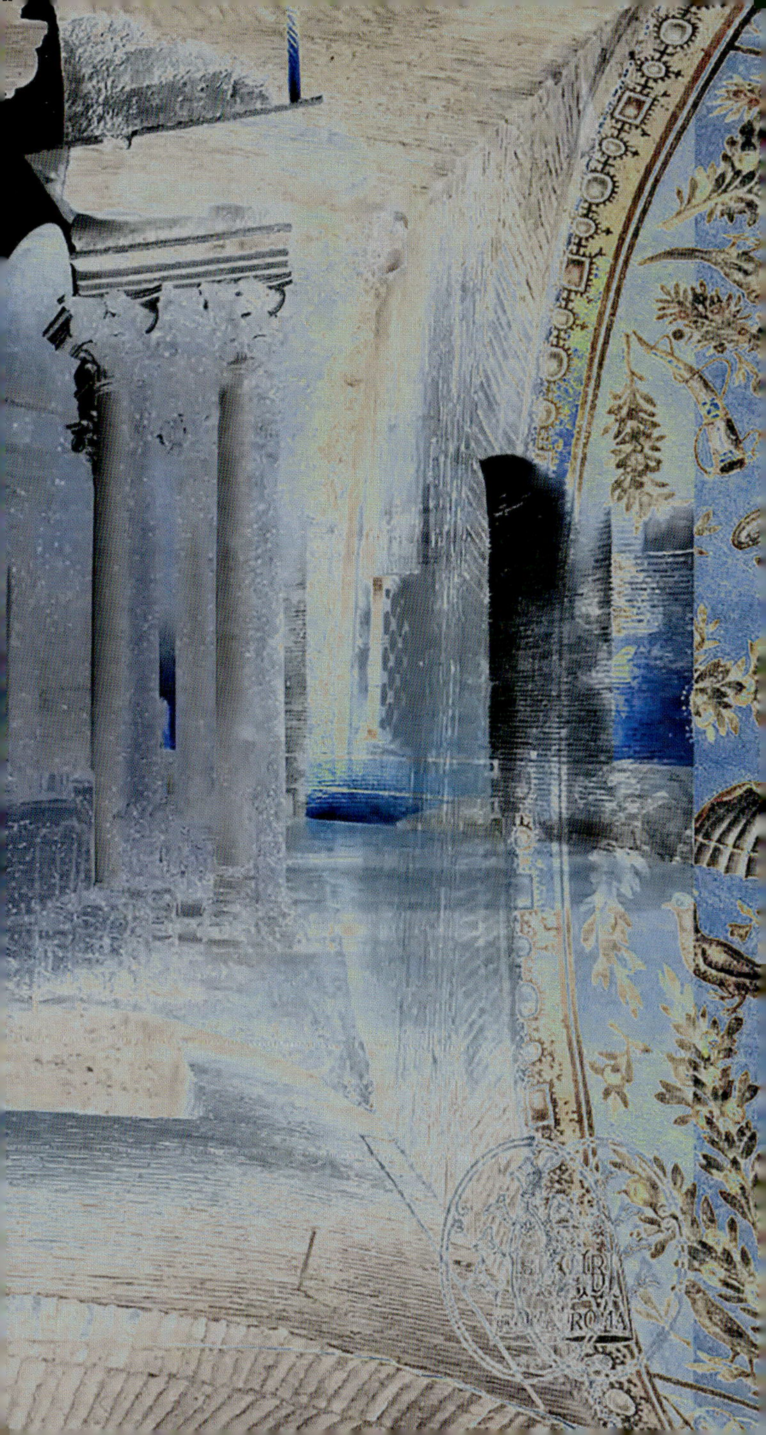

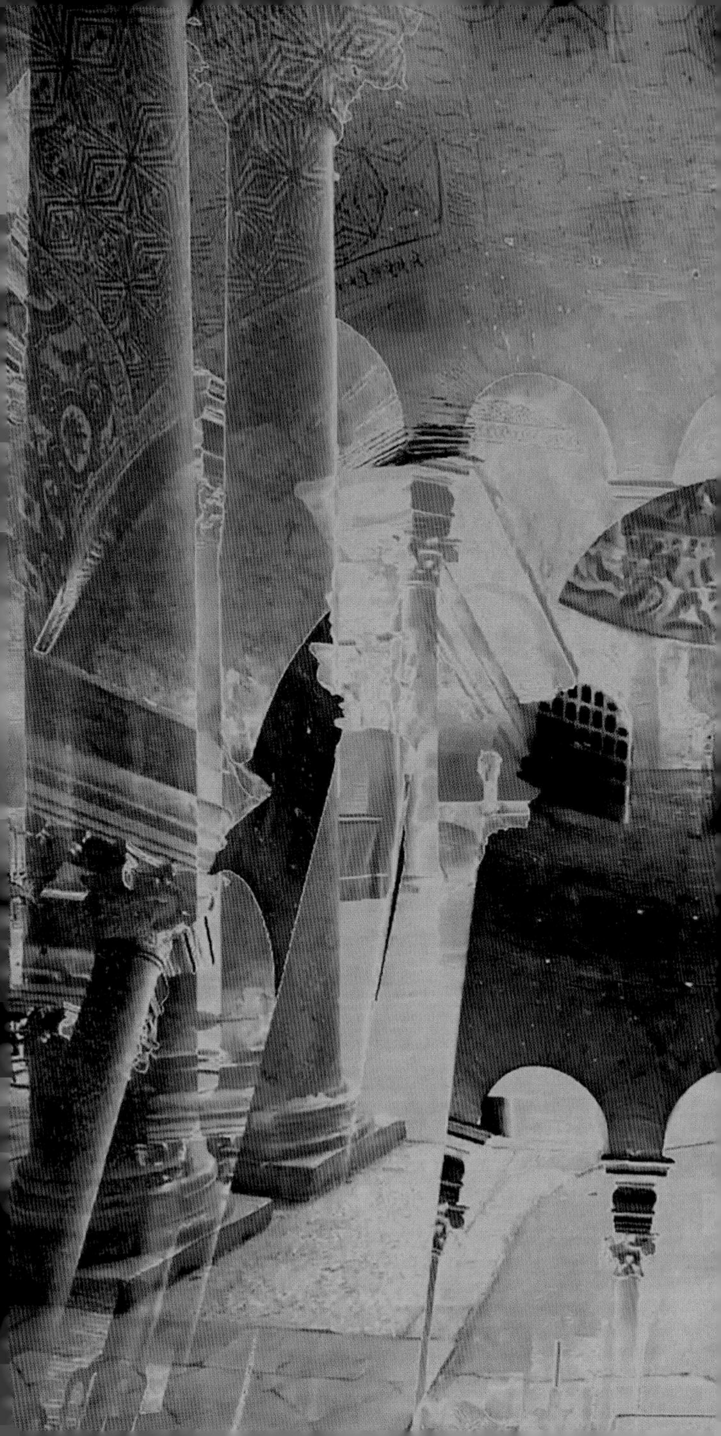

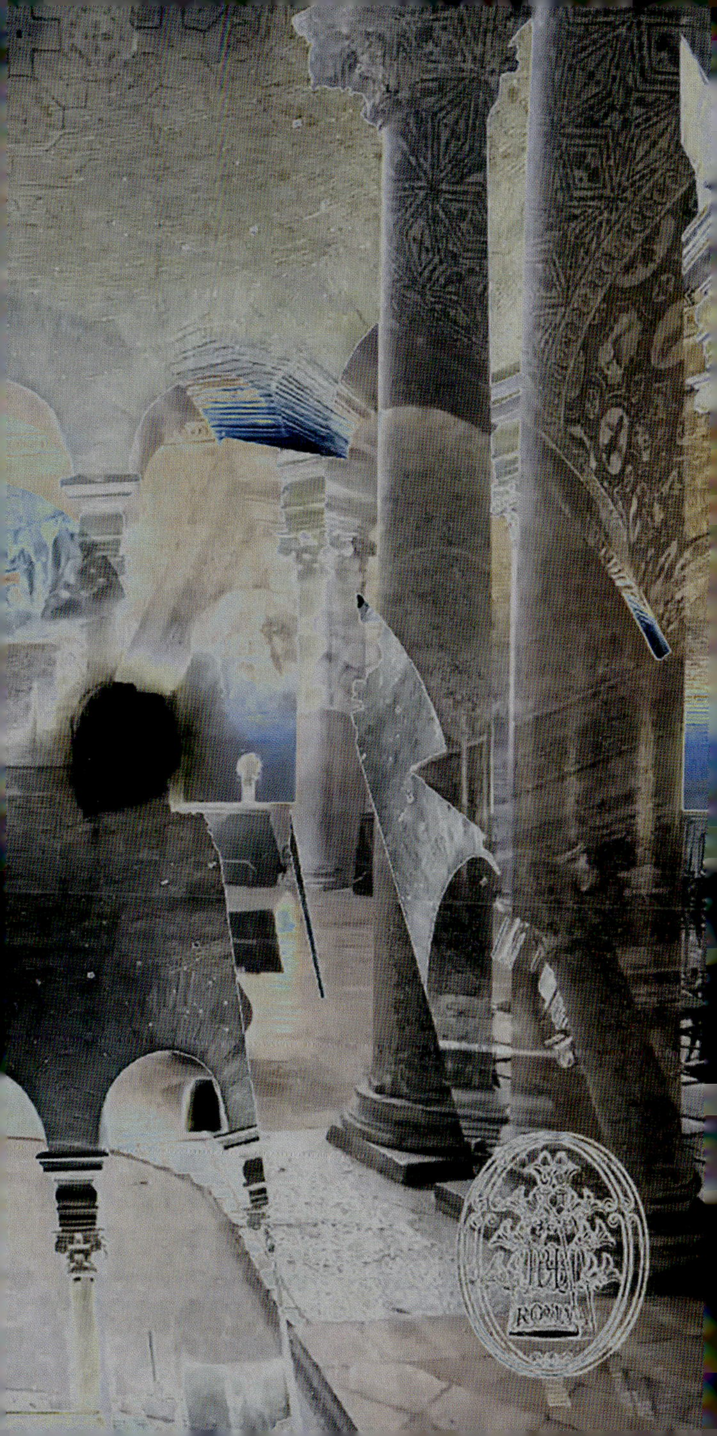

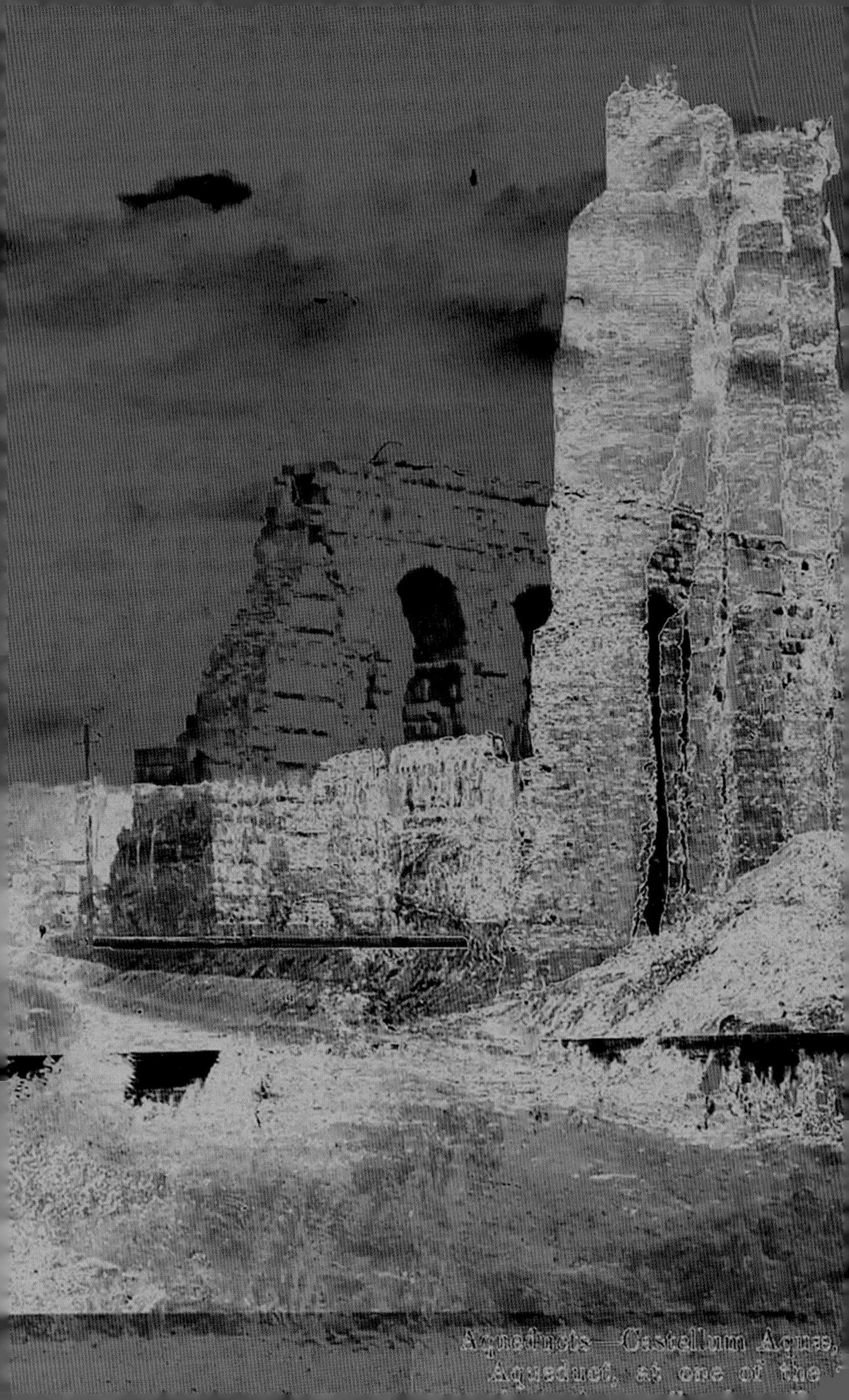

Aqueducts.—Castellum Aquæ,
Aqueduct, at one of the

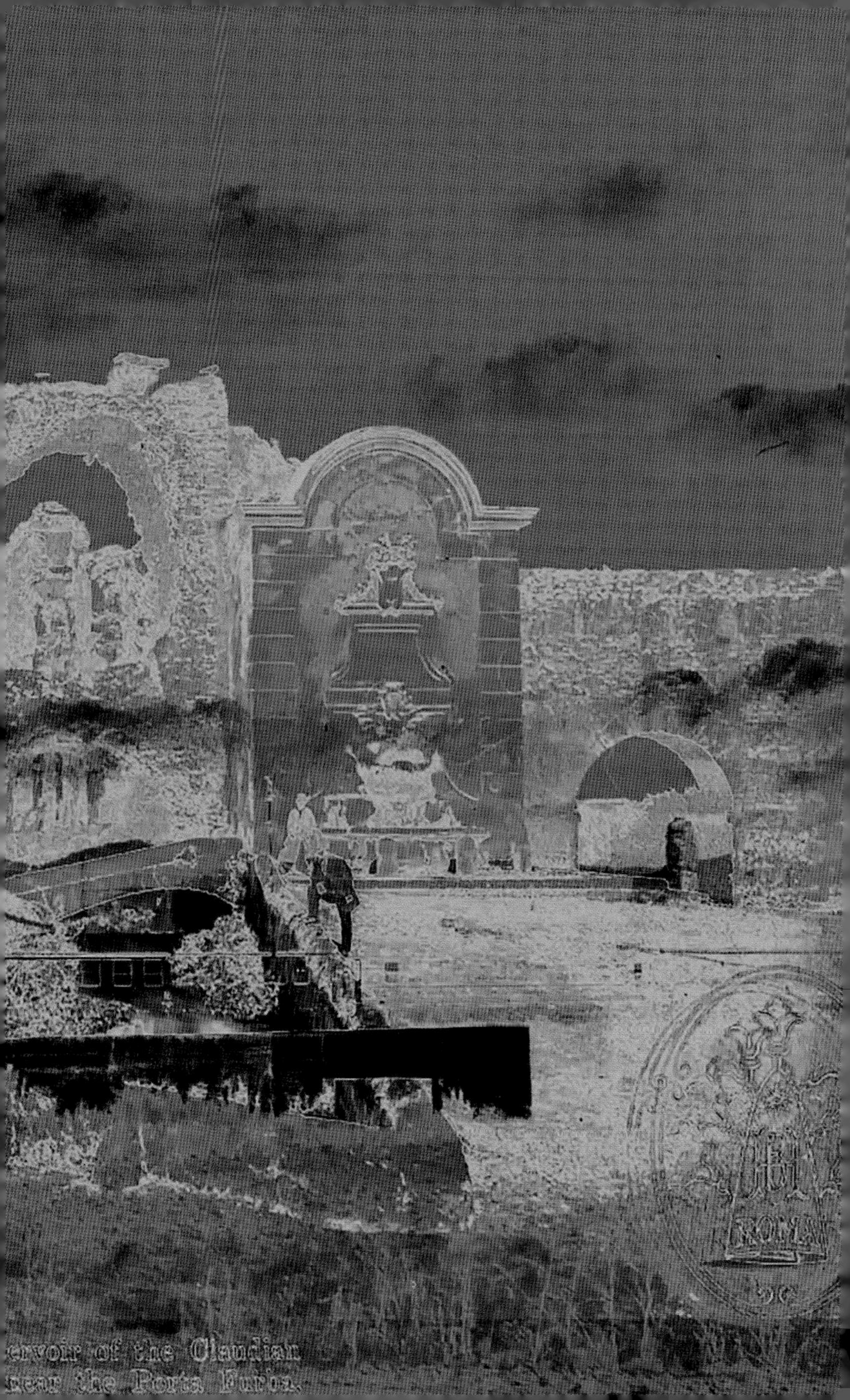

ervoir of the Claudian
near the Porta Furba.

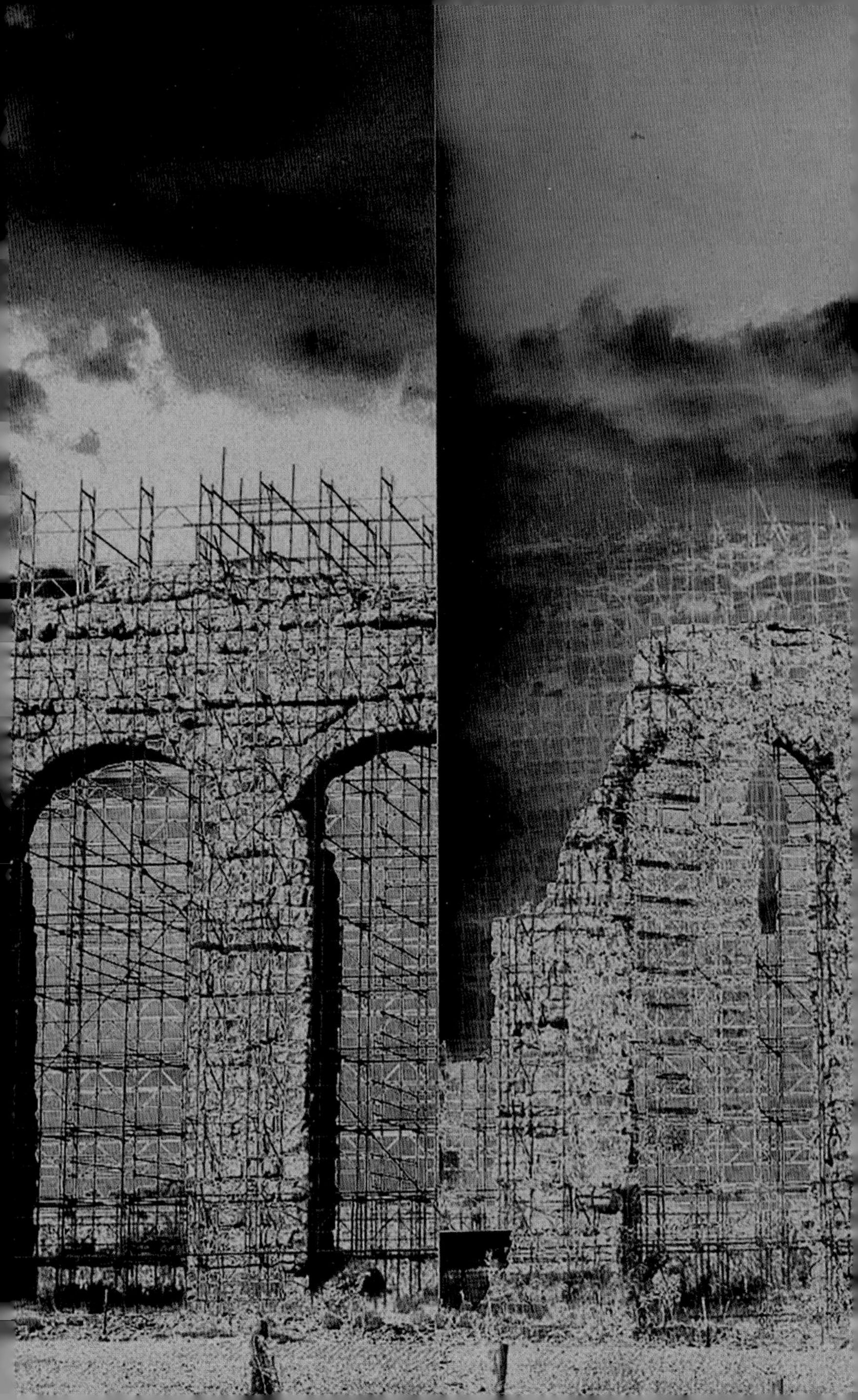

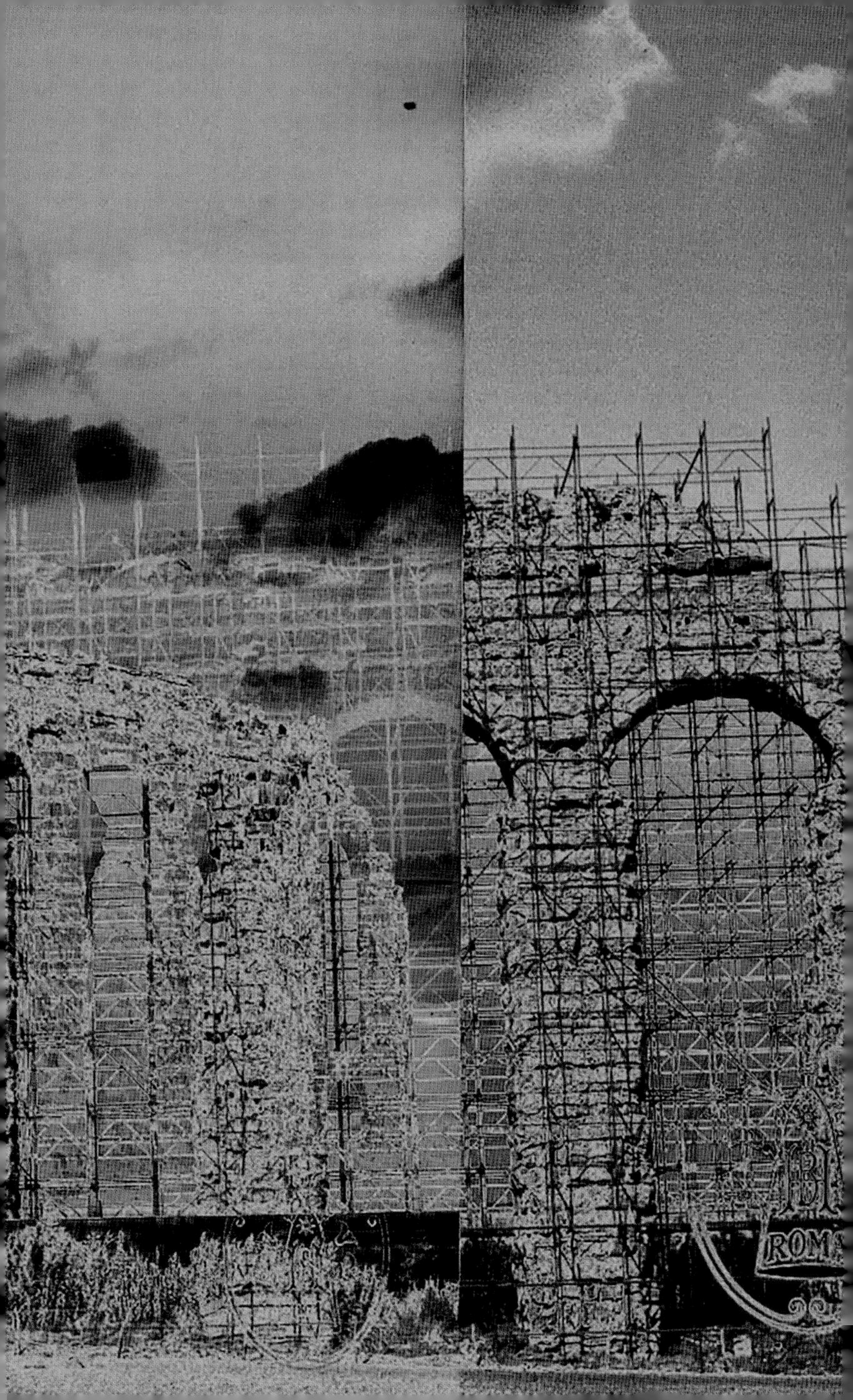

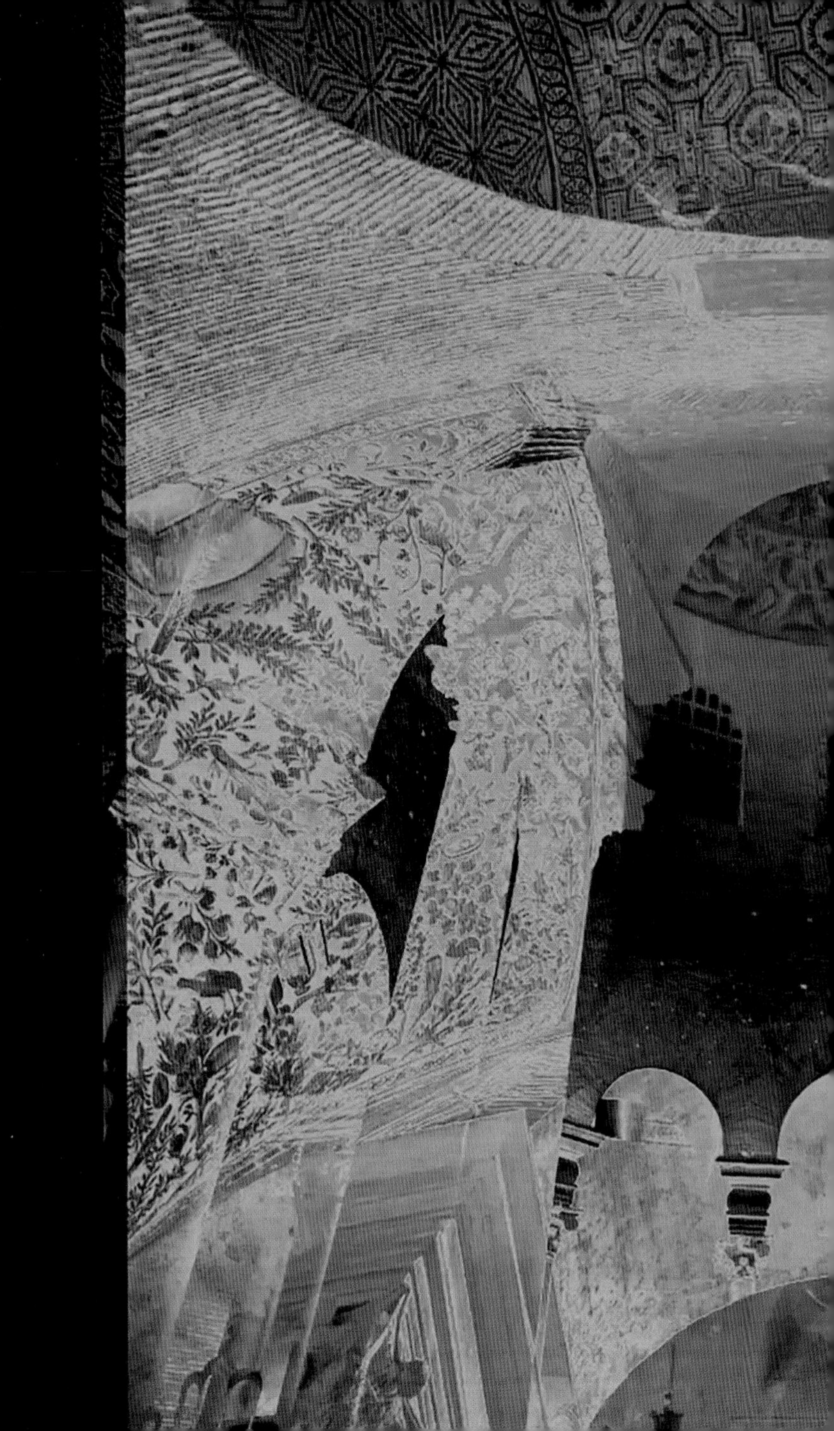

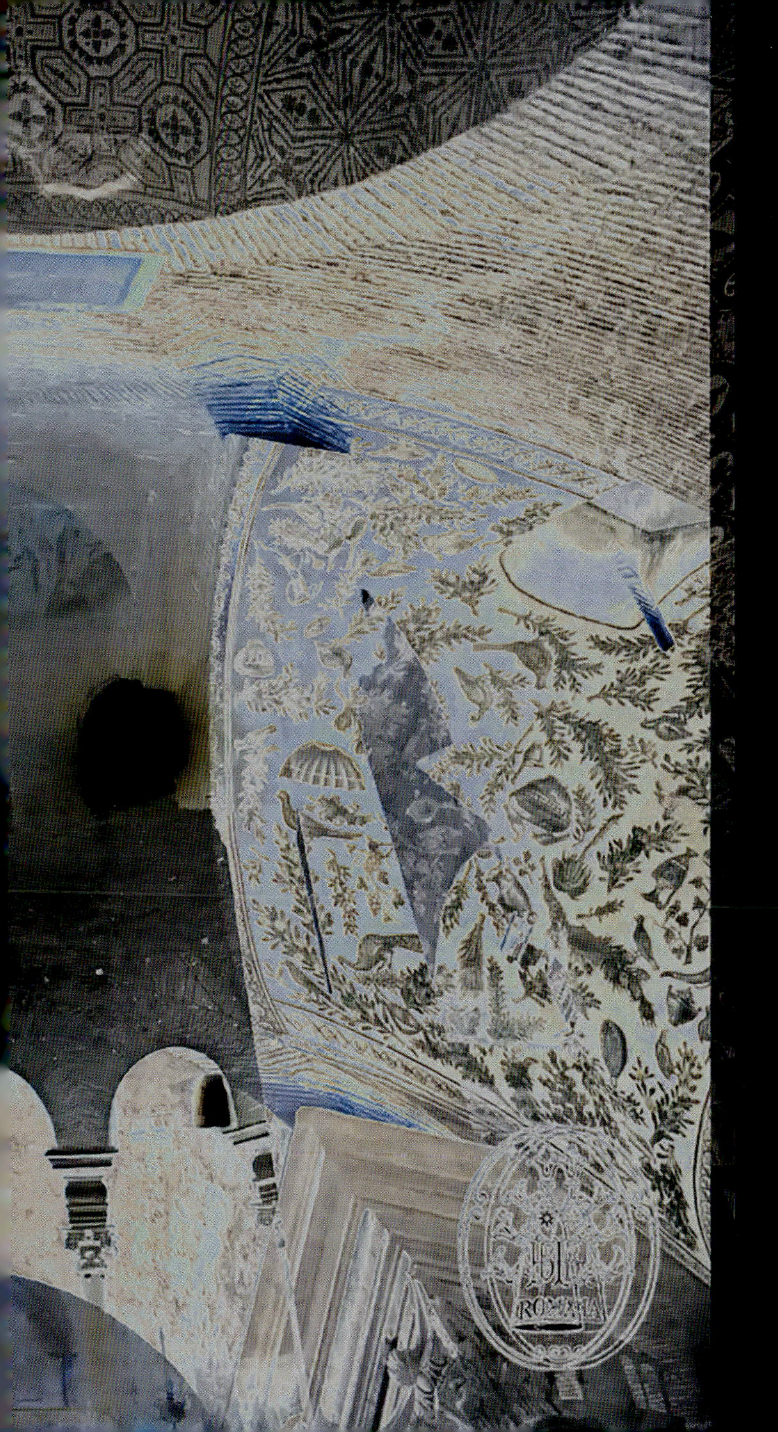

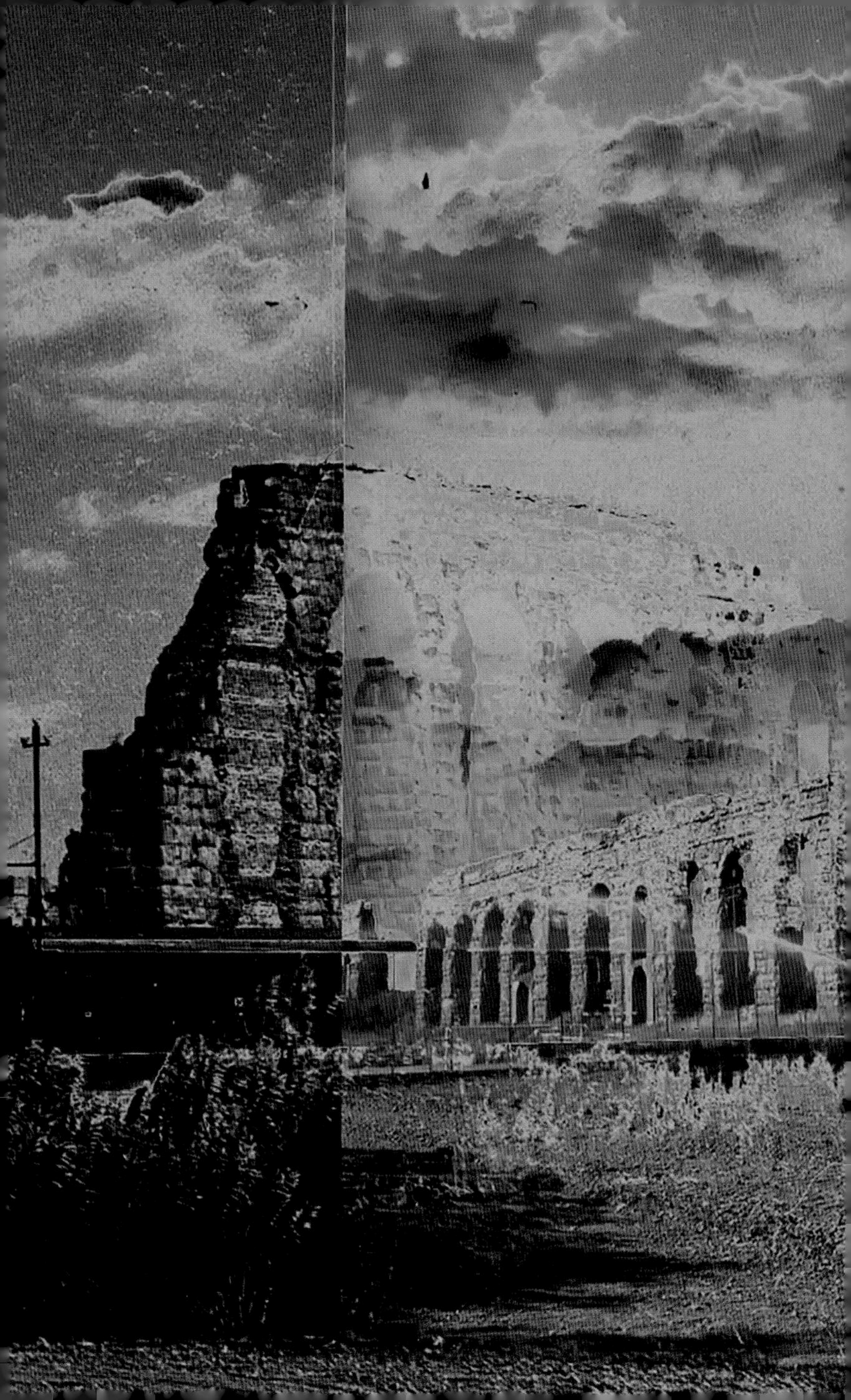

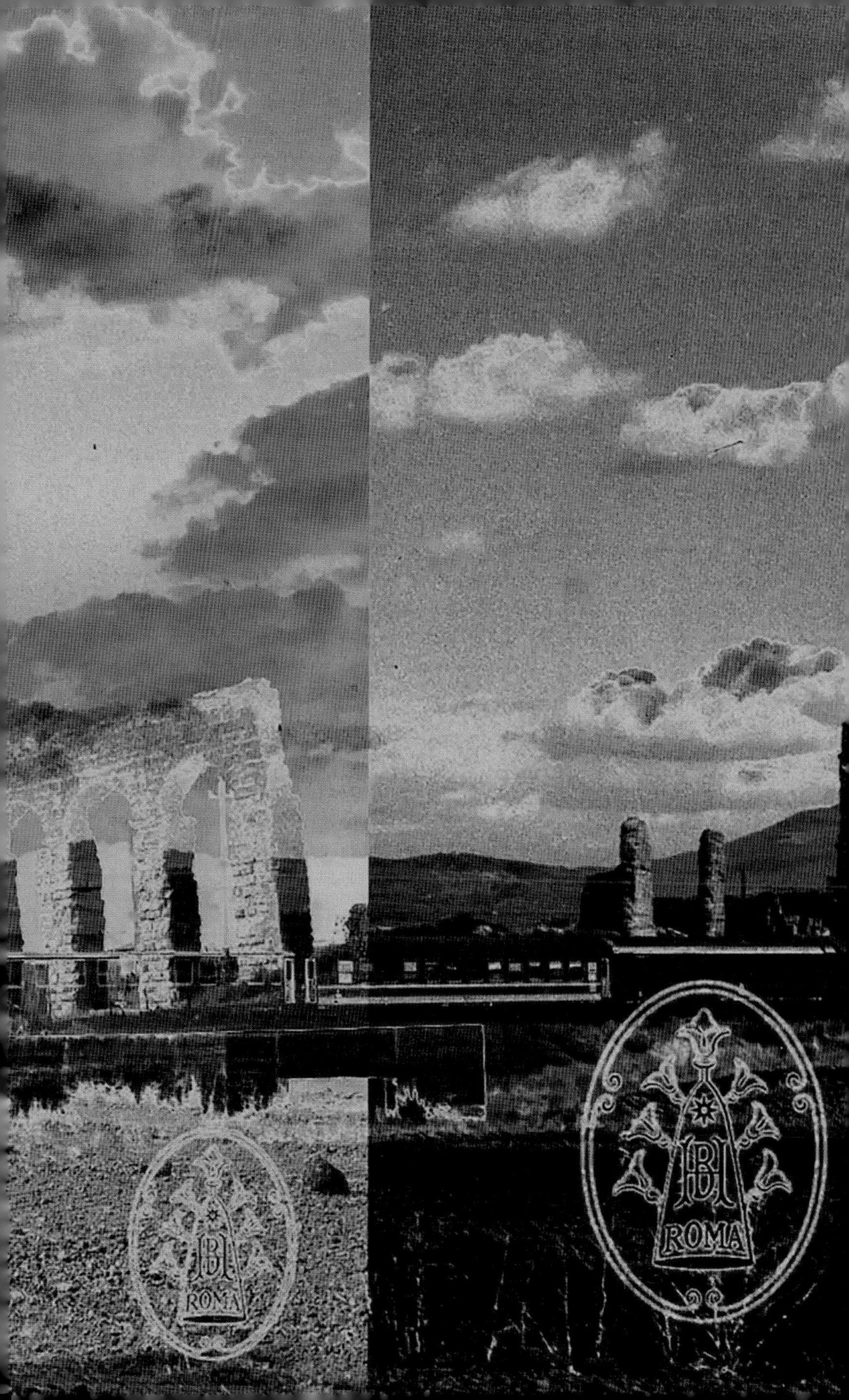
ROMA
ROMA

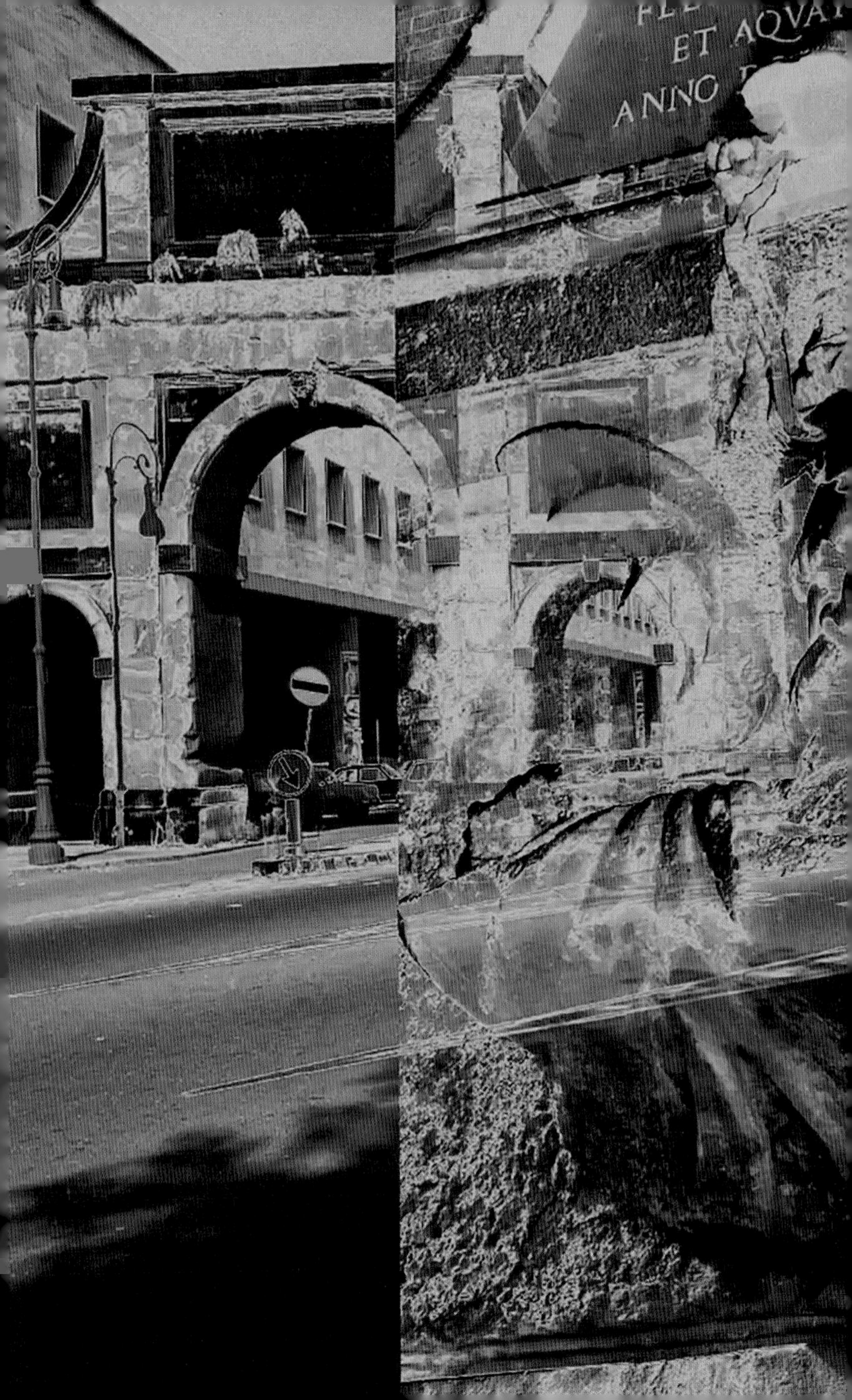

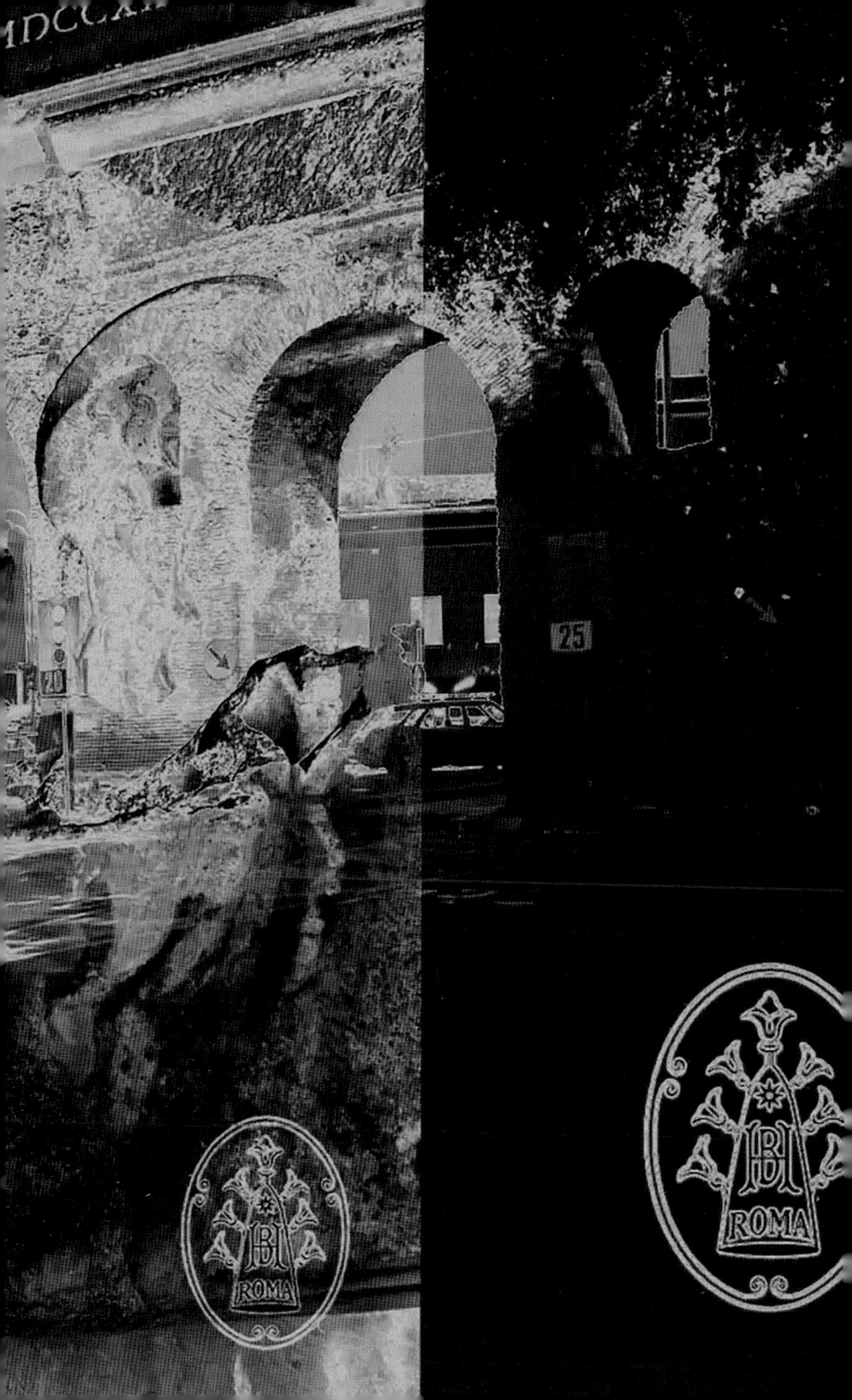
25
20
ROMA
ROMA

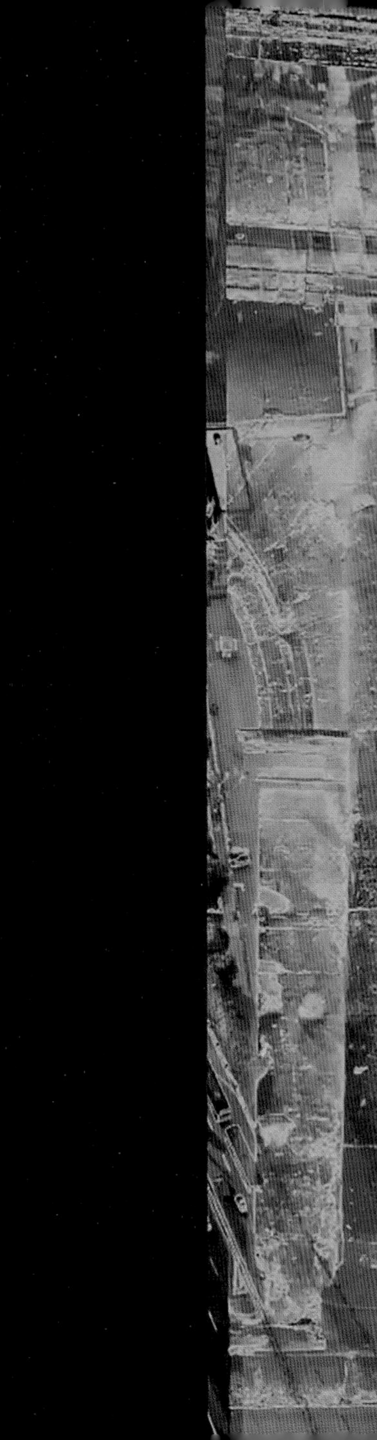

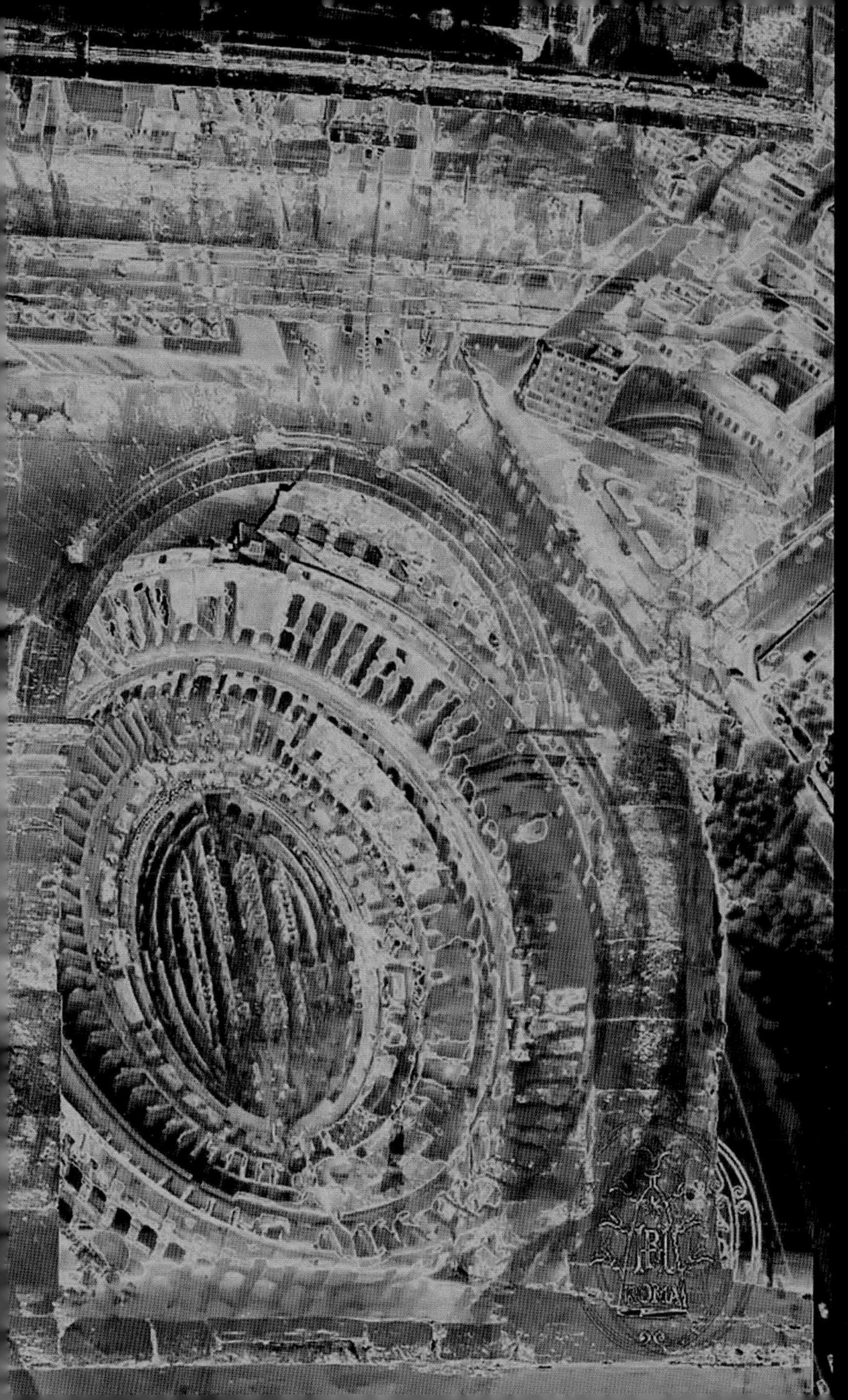
ROMA

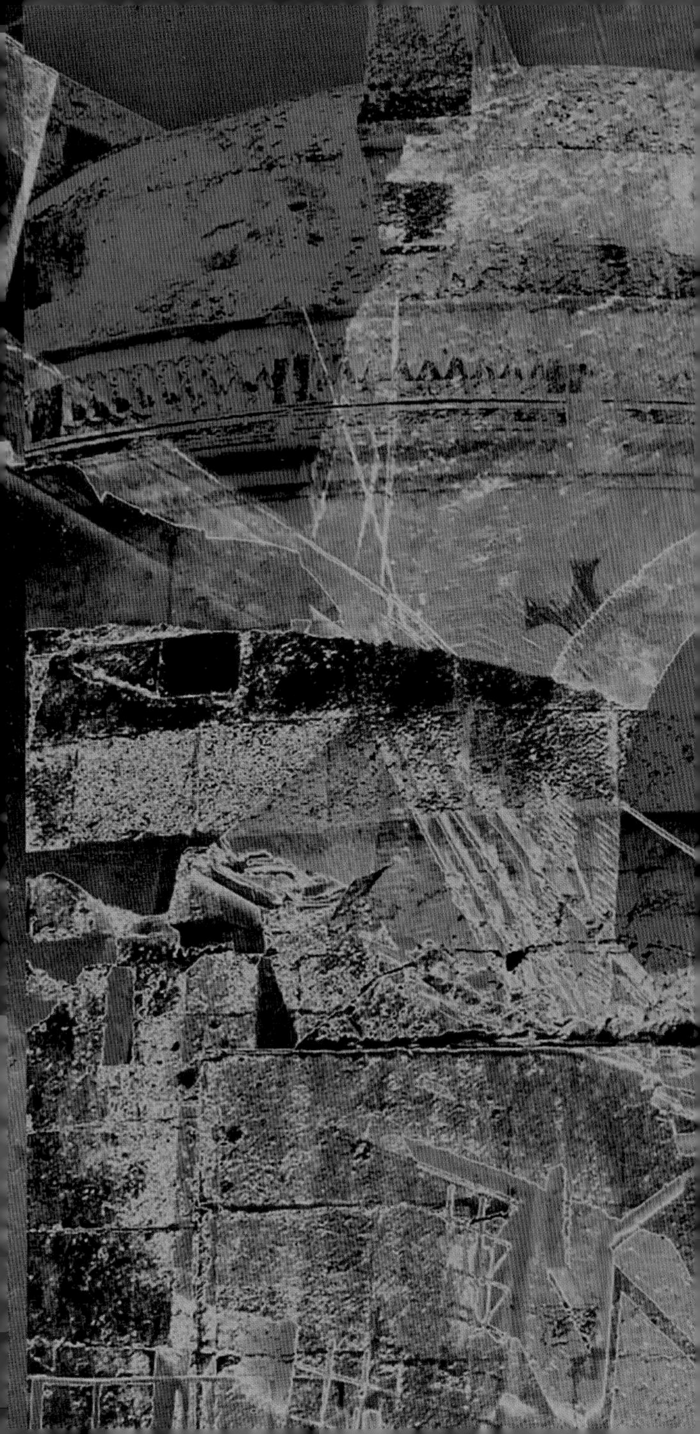

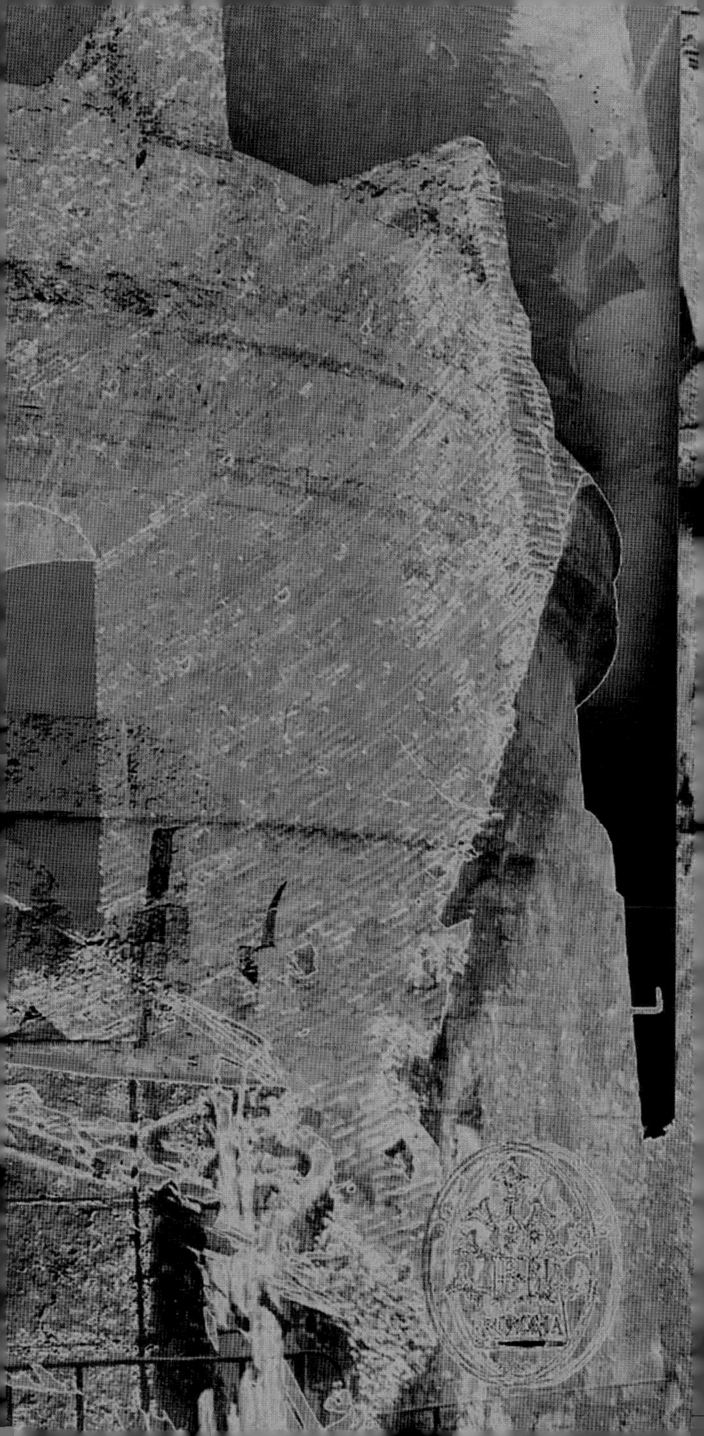

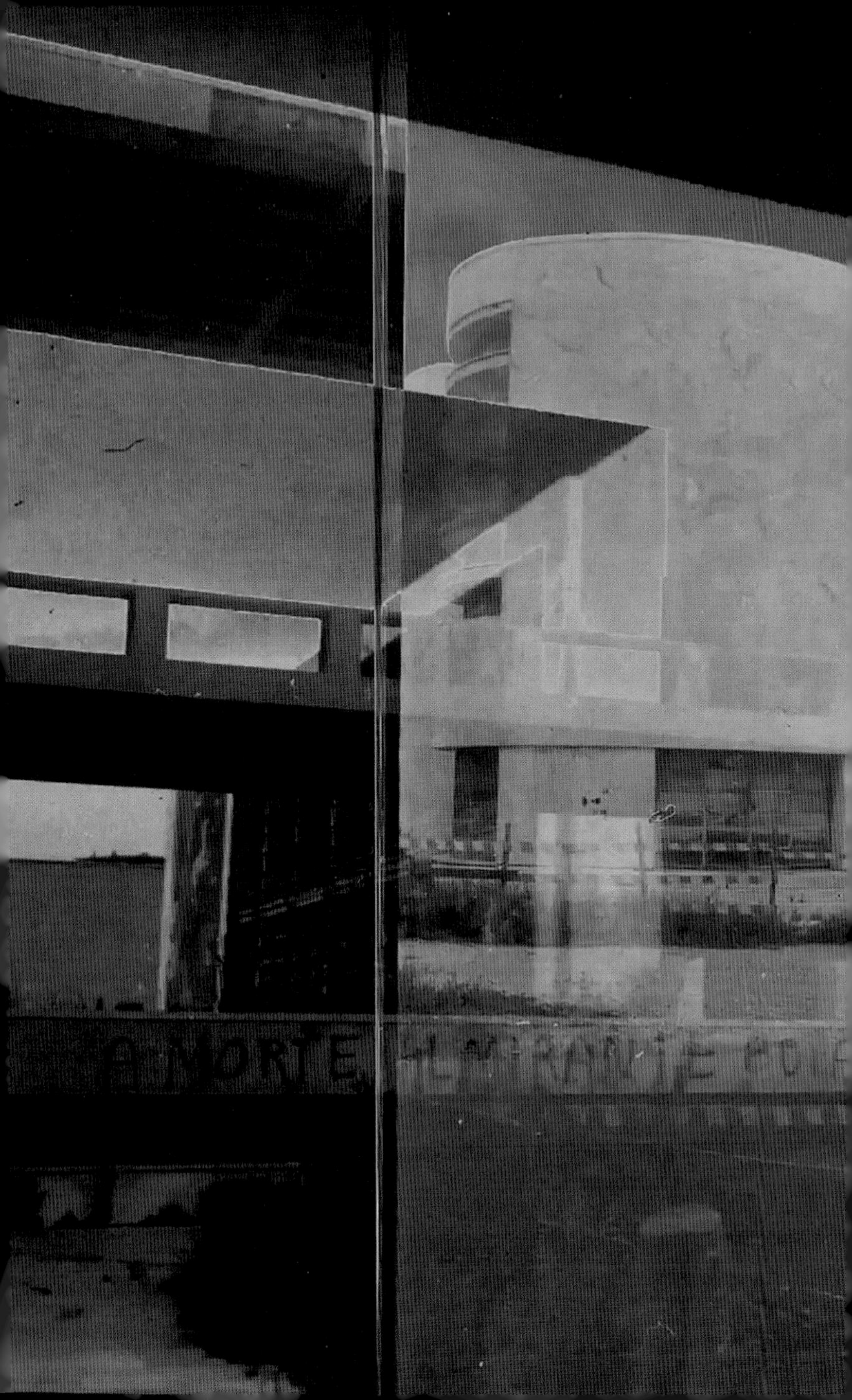
A NORTE

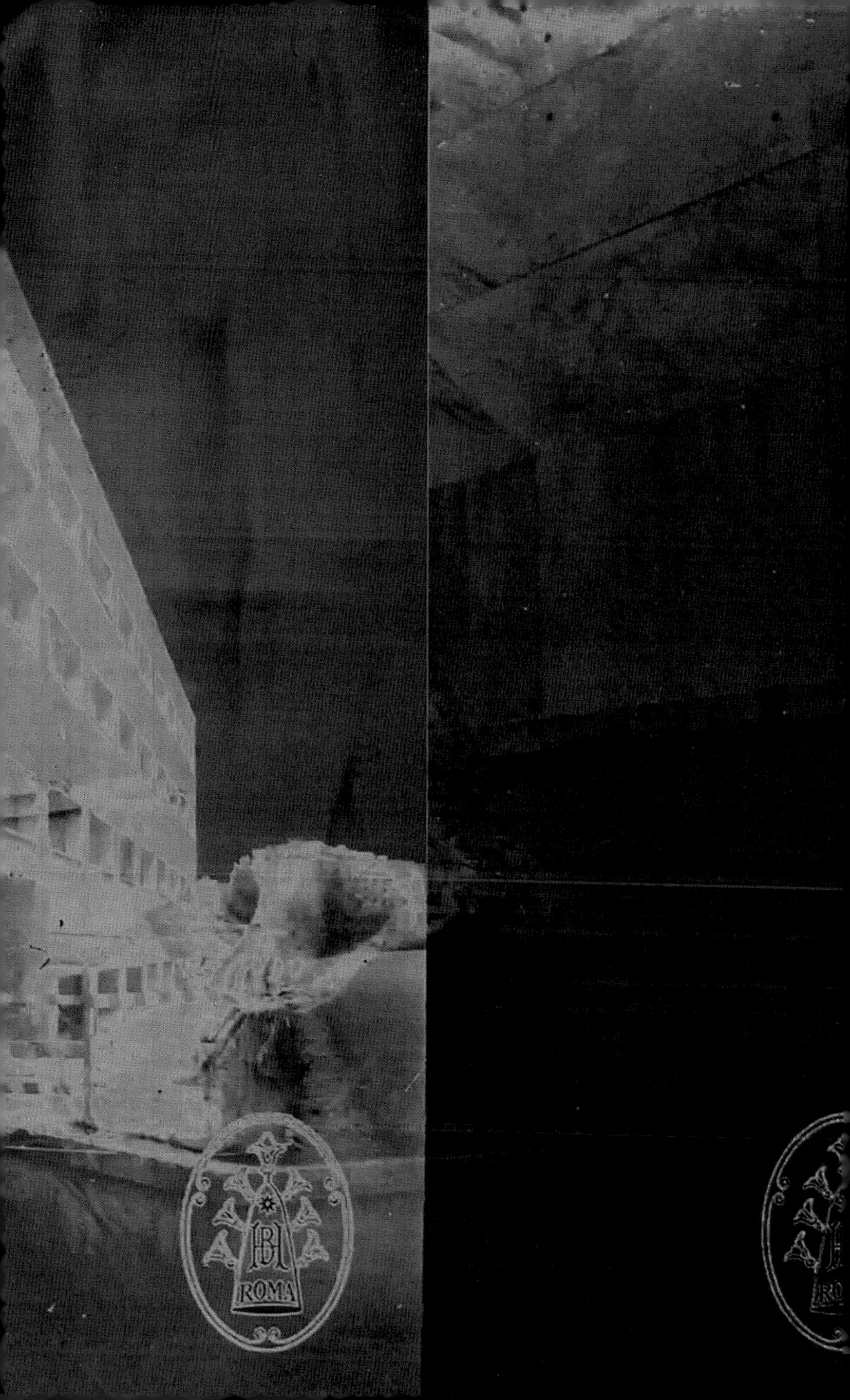
ROMA

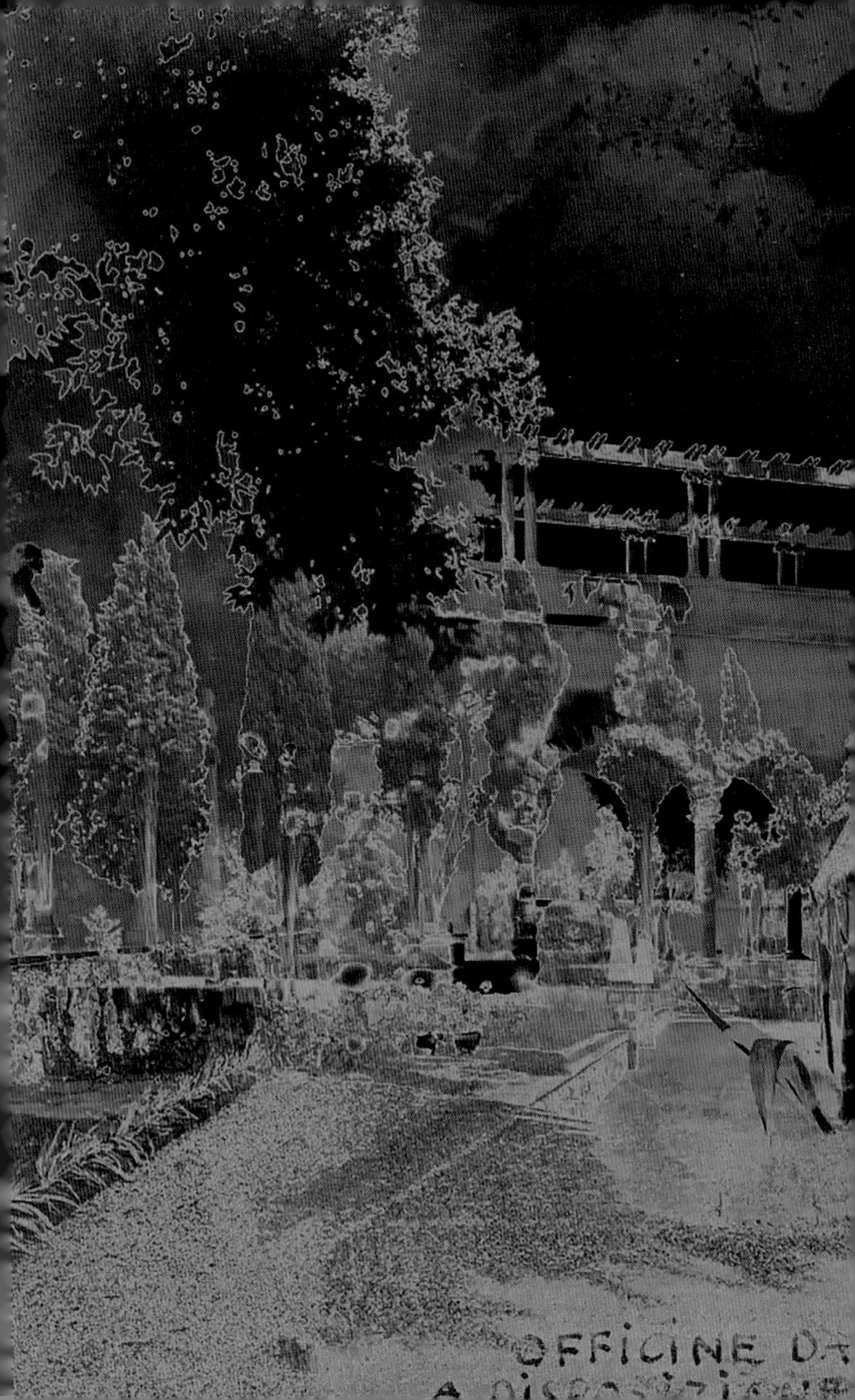
OFFICINE

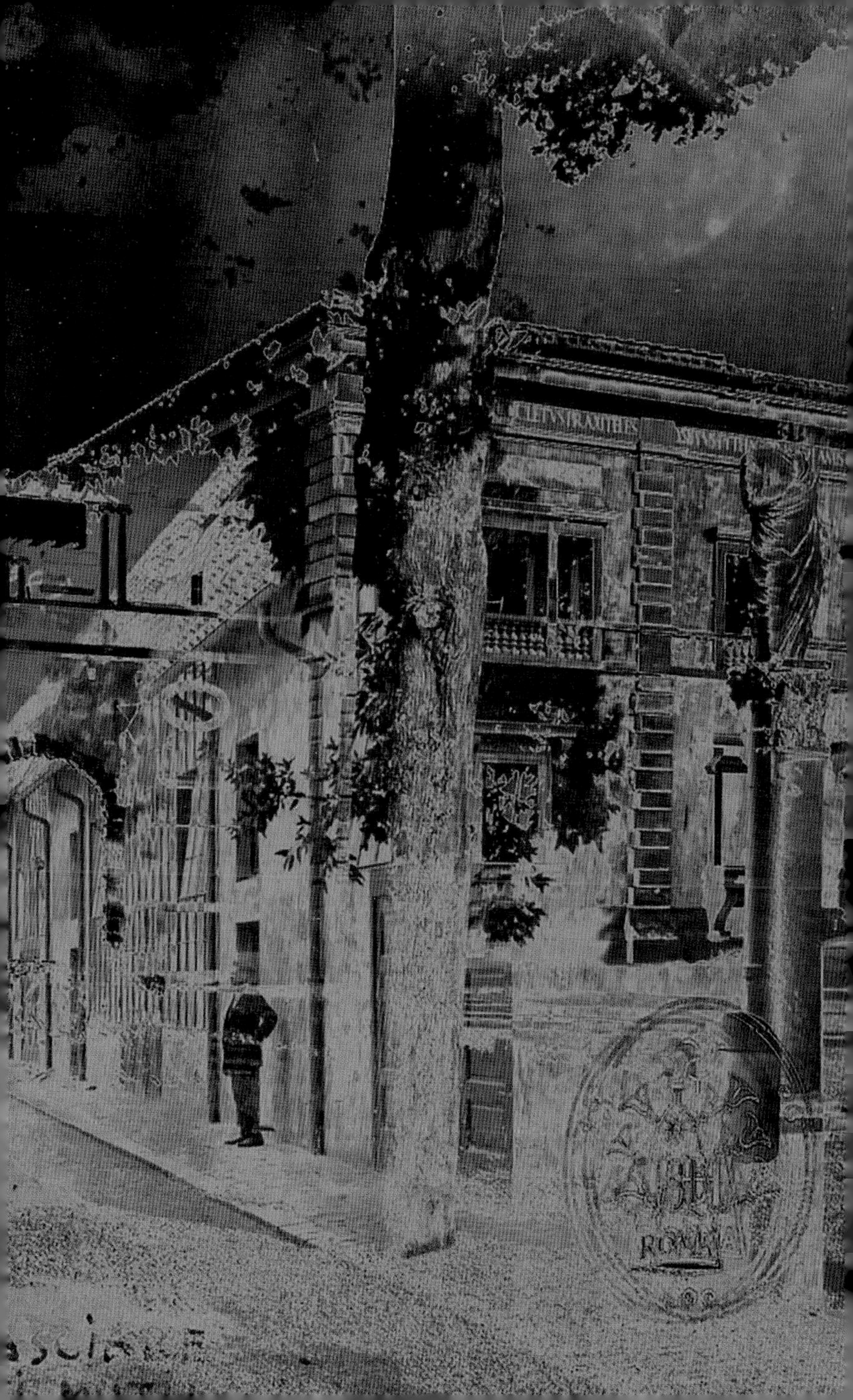

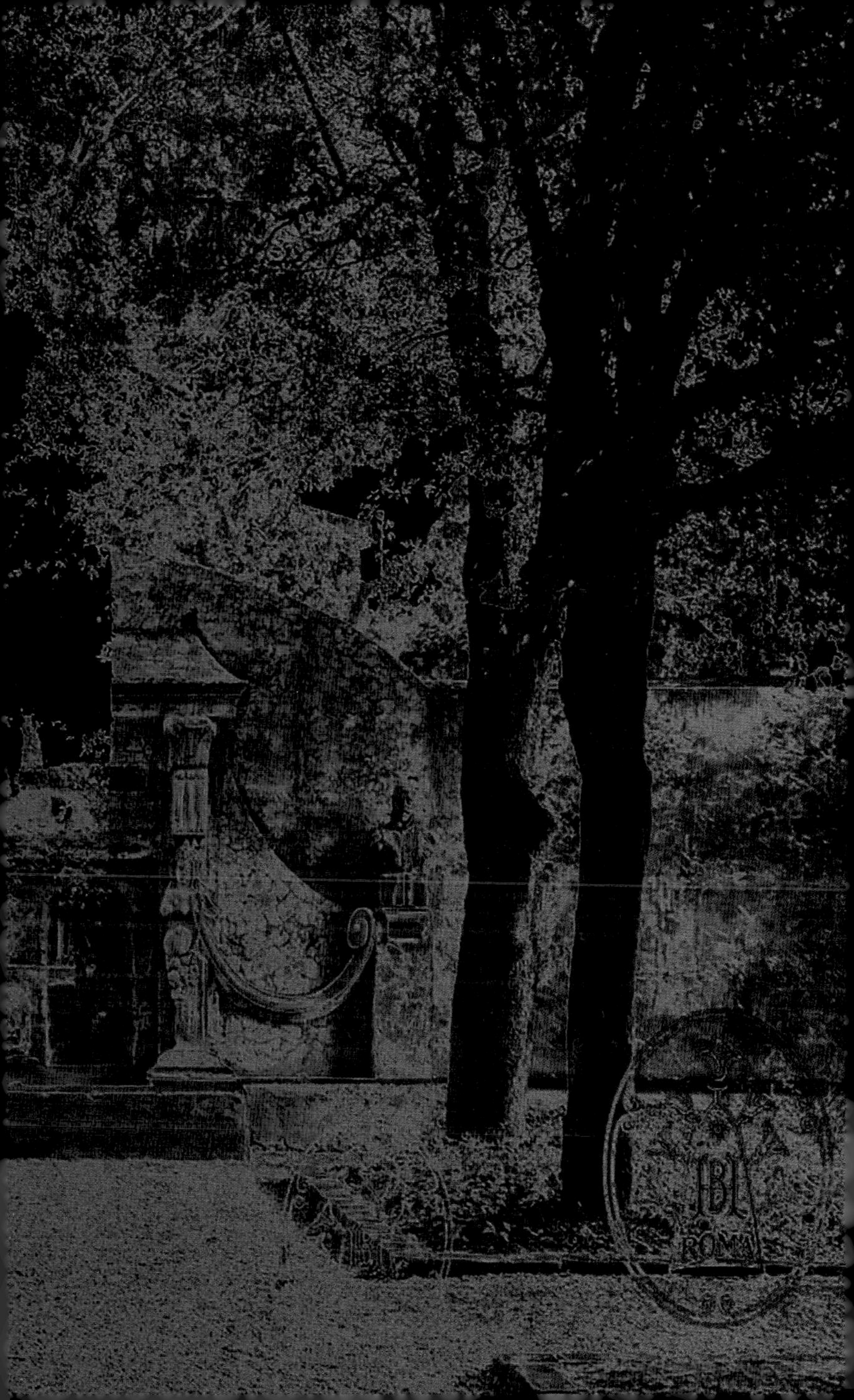

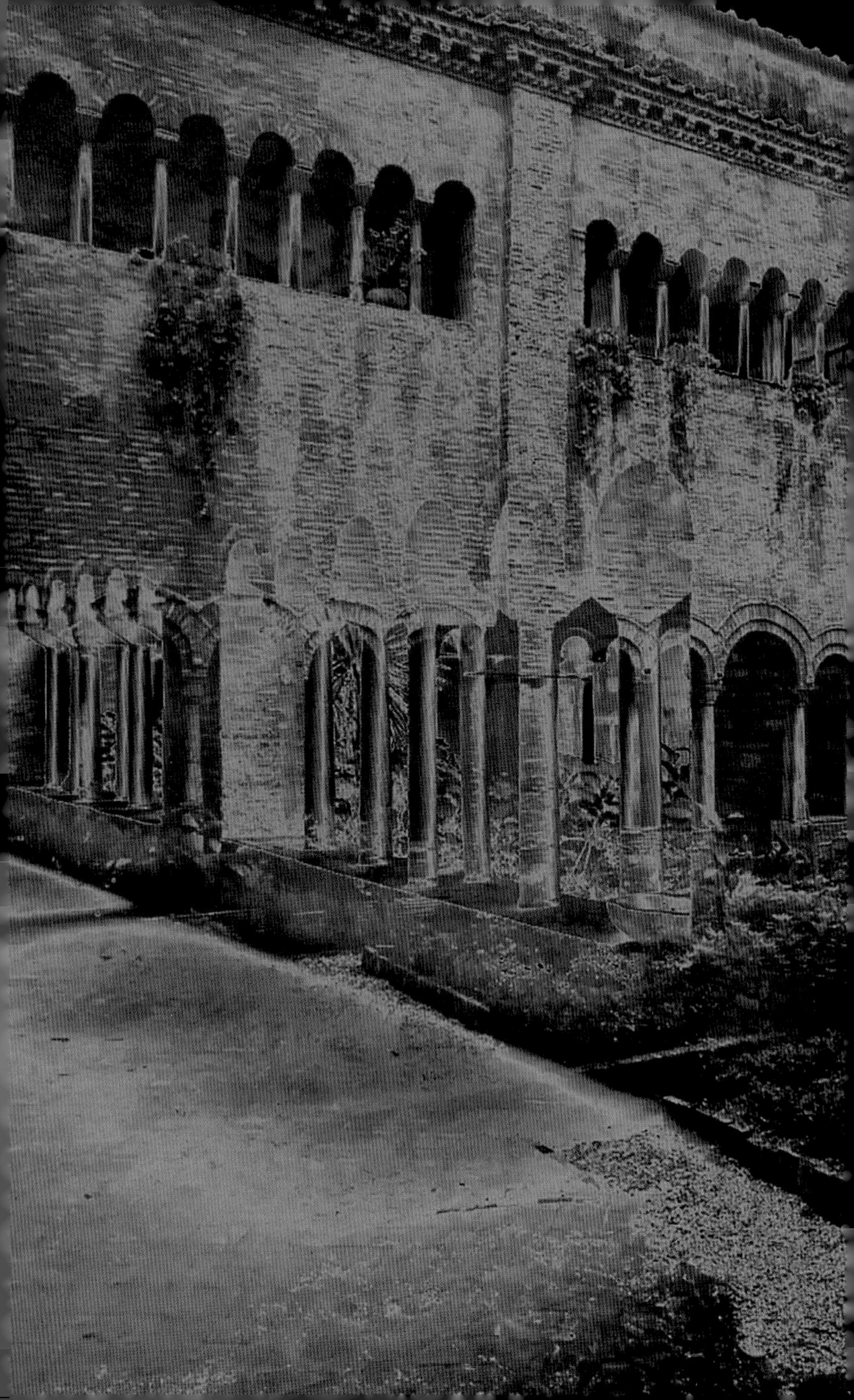

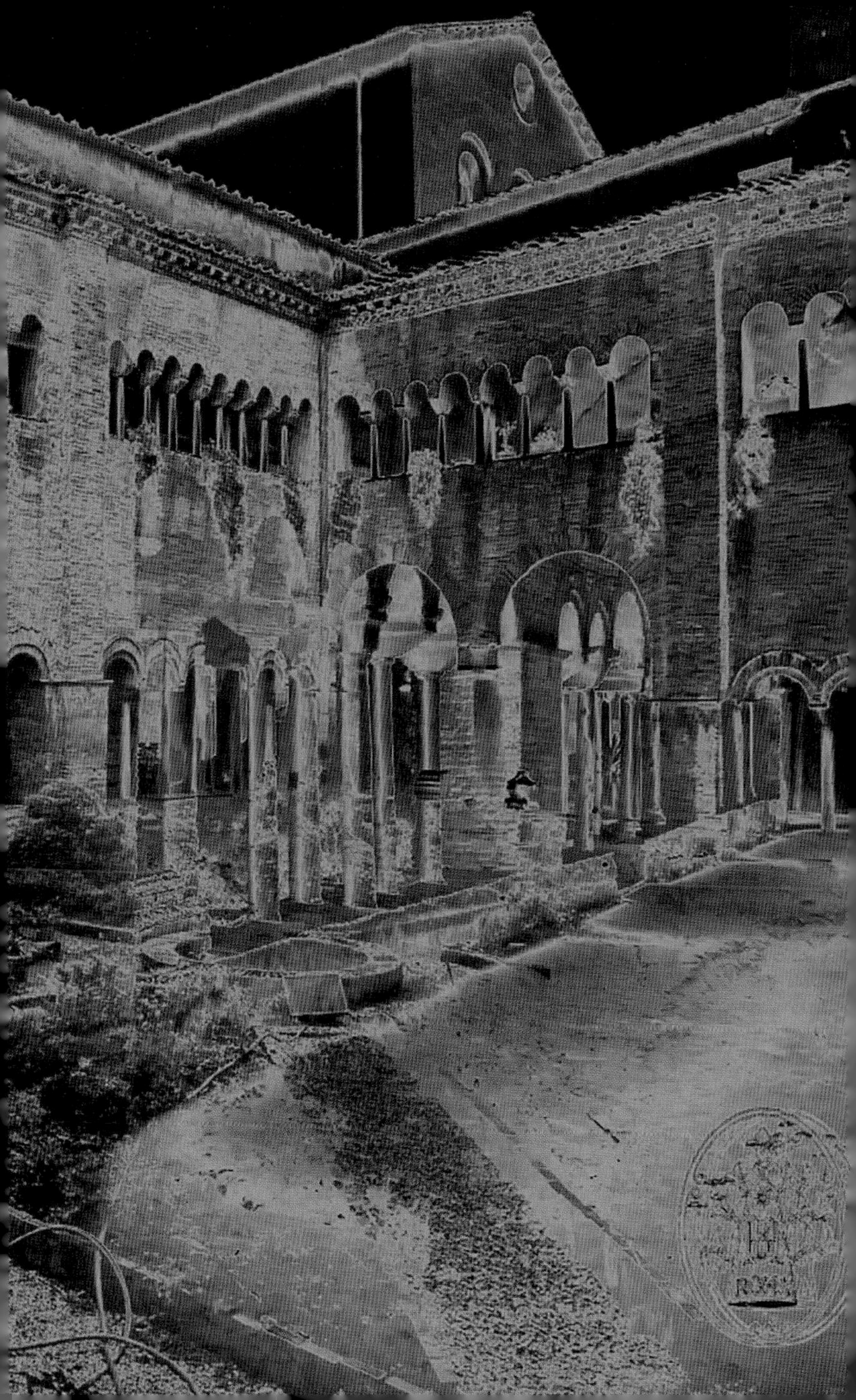

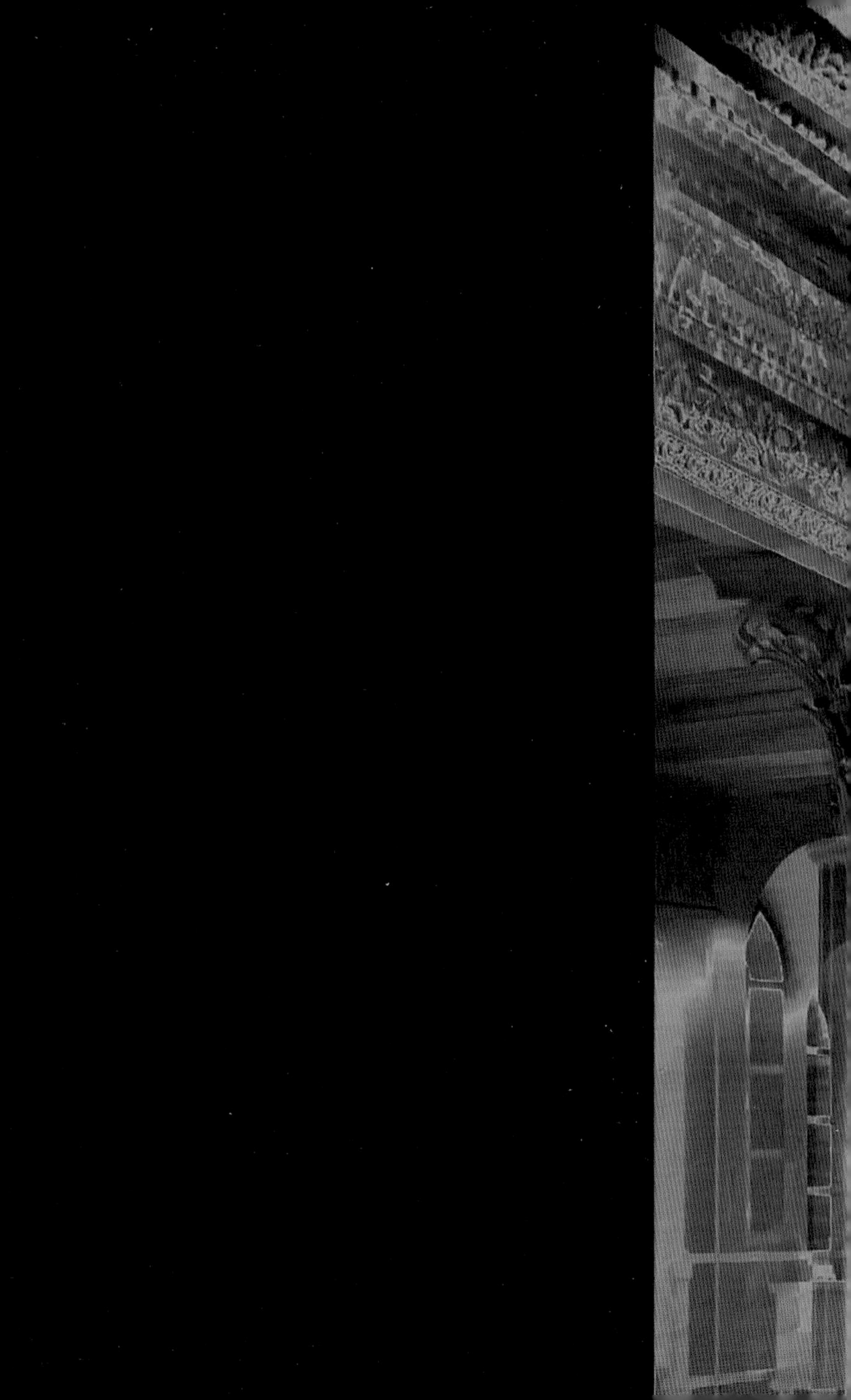

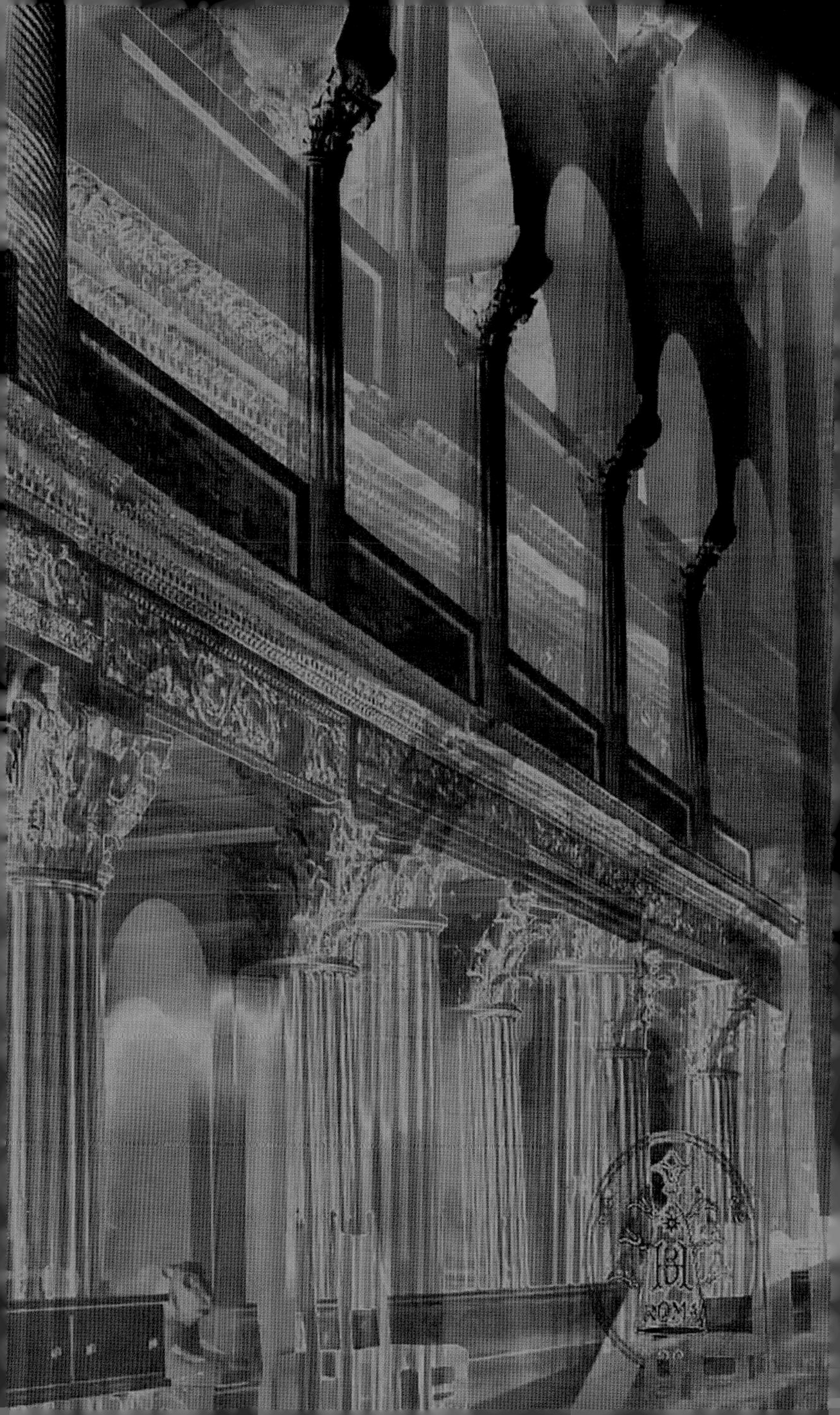
ROMA

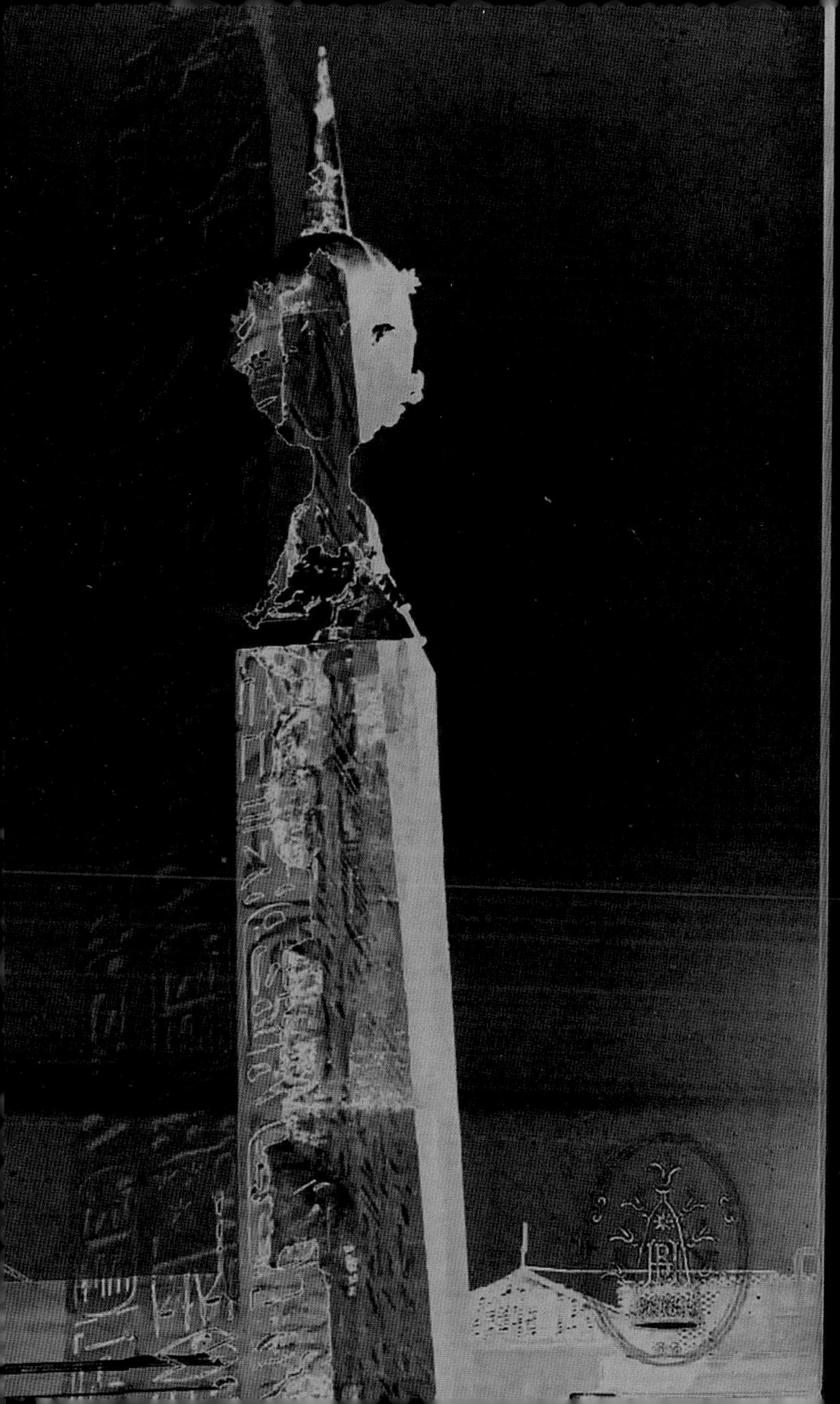

The contributions by Carolin Kosuch and Maria Clara Martinelli are based on research interviews conducted by the author in 2018 at the German Historical Institute in Rome and the Luigi Bernabò Brea Archaeological Museum in Lipari, Aeolian Islands, Italy.

Carolin Kosuch is a historian of modern history at the University of Göttingen. At the German Historical Institute in Rome, she researched the German-Italian cultural history of cremation in the nineteenth century.

Maria Clara Martinelli is an archaeologist working at the Luigi Bernabò Brea Archaeological Museum in Lipari on the Aeolian Islands. Her research focuses on the prehistory of the Mediterranean.

The image series presented in the back of the book are collages composed of archival materials originating from the Photographic Collection at the Bibliotheca Hertziana – Max Planck Institute for Art History in Rome that were superimposed and artistically processed further by the author. They are based on stills from the film DOPOSTORIA.

Cover Photograph: View from the cemetery of the Aeolian island of Lipari toward the "Rocca Rossa," or red rock, with the Archaeological Museum and the island of Vulcano in the background. Christoph Keller, 2018.

Christoph Keller:
DOPOSTORIA

Edited by Christoph Keller

Copy editing and translations by Alisa Lieu Kotmair, Ben Bazalgette, Caspar Shaller, Julia Triolo

Line editing and proofreading by George MacBeth, Claudia Kotte, Mirko Gatti, Courtney Johnson

Transcriptions by Caterina Flor Gümpel, Pauline Wessel

Graphic design by
Studio Manuel Raeder
(Lucas Liccini, Manuel Raeder)

Printed in Germany by Vier-Türme GmbH, Benedict Press

Edition of 1000

Published by

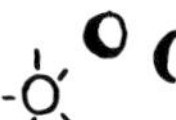

BOM
DIA
BOA
TARDE
BOA
NOITE

Rosa-Luxemburg-Strasse 17
10178 Berlin, Germany
www.bomdiabooks.de

ISBN 978-3-96436-066-3

The Deutsche Nationalbibliothek lists this publication in the Deutsche National-bibliografie; detailed bibliographic data are available on the internet at http://dnb.dnb.de.

Funded by the Berlin Artistic Research Grant Programme and supported by the Berlin Senate Department for Culture and Europe. Thanks to Rike Frank and Kathrin Busch.

berliner förderprogramm künstlerische forschung

Senatsverwaltung für Kultur und Europa | BERLIN

We would also like to thank the following people and institutions: Bibliotheca Hertziana – Max Planck Institute for Art History in Rome, Tristan Weddigen, Tanja Michalsky, Golo Maurer; Ilaria Bussoni, Il mondo in fine, Galleria Nazionale d'Arte Moderna Roma; Esther Schipper Berlin; Fondazione Catel in Rome; the Photographic Collection of the Bibliotheca Hertziana, Johannes Röll, Tatjana Bartsch, and Irmgard Palladino; Villa Massimo in Rome; Philine Helas, Maria Bremer, Maria Teresa Costa, Toni Hildebrandt, Beate Thomas, and Isabelle Moffat; Haytham El Wardany, Jumana Manna, Natascha Sadr Haghighian, and Ute Waldhausen; Bad Muskau and Mini-Makhsoos, Berlin.